Doomed To Be Nothing, Destined To Be Something

By Marsha Woodland

Doomed To Be Nothing, Destined To Be Something

© Copyright 2011 Marsha Woodland

All rights reserved. This book is protected under the copyright laws of the United States of America. No portion of this book may be reproduced in any form, without the written permission of the publisher. Permission granted on request.

Unlock Publishing House
231 West Hampton Place
Capitol Heights, MD 20743
www.unlockpublishinghouse.com
1 (240) 619-3852

Cover designed by Becca Rodgers

Unlock Publishing House is not responsible for any content or determination of work. All information is solely considered as the point of view of the author.

ISBN: 978-0-9829318-9-9

This is the story of one girl's journey from incest, molestation, rape and domestic violence to deliverance, freedom and liberation.

A real-life nightmare turned fairytale…

Dedication

I would like to dedicate this book to my dear mother; the late Barbara Jean Woodland Bakr', for she truly is my inspiration.

I would like to thank my beautiful children, Tarika, Tavares, Tasha and Taliyah, as well as Robert; I love you guys for standing by me and with me during my dry seasons.

I salute my siblings, Clarence, Winslow, Doris, Derrick and Jeremiah for being there in good and bad times, and for doing your parts to keep our mother's legacy alive.

To my spiritual and church families, I never would have made it without you; you know who you are. Betty Hastings, Elder Ronald and Dr. Andree Murphy I love you; and may god continue to use, bless and keep you all.

My heart felt gratitude goes out to God first, Tawnya Lee, Rachel Grant, Gregorio Clarke, Anita Perry, Becca Rogers, Alicia S., and Liesa Ricks for always being there.

Last but not least, I would like to say with love and sincerity, thank you to my dad for expecting so much of me, and to my stepmother and sister; thanks for never giving up on me.

Doomed to be Nothing, Destined to be Something

Table of Contents

Foreword 13
Chapter 1 15
Chapter 2 19
Chapter 3 23
Chapter 4 27
Chapter 5 33
Chapter 6 37
Chapter 7 41
Chapter 8 45
Chapter 9 51
Chapter 10 57
Chapter 11 61
Chapter 12 65
Chapter 13 71
Chapter 14 75
Chapter 15 79
Chapter 16 83
Chapter 17 87
Chapter 18 91
Chapter 19 95
Chapter 20 99
Chapter 21 105
Chapter 22 109
Chapter 23 113
Chapter 24 119
Chapter 25 123
Chapter 26 129
Chapter 27 133
Chapter 28 139
Chapter 29 145
Chapter 30 149
Chapter 31 153
Chapter 32 157
Reflections 159

Doomed to be Nothing, Destined to be Something

Foreword

Doomed to be Nothing, Destined to be Something is a prime example of 'I shall not die but live.' As Marsha Woodland labored over this book, I watched the caterpillar push through a painful cocoon and erupt into a beautiful butterfly. It gladdens my heart to see the move of God in this book. If you are holding this book in your hand and you've experienced a dark and frightened past, unleash the bondage of your past, be ready to move forward into your rightful place and allow the spirit of love and forgiveness to become your closest friend. Through this book I believe that hope will be restored to the hopeless, faith to the faithless, and freedom to those in bondage. Ultimately after reading this book one can come to believe that they too have a destiny and it's not doomed.

I applaud Marsha Woodland for this wonderful work that will be used to glorify God.

Dr. Andrée M. Harris

Doomed to be Nothing, Destined to be Something

Chapter 1

Rebecca's life has been anything but a bed of roses and white picket fences. While other little girls ran and played, she sat and got fingered. Yes, fingered. While they slept at night, she was raped. It began when she was about 4 or 5 years old and undoubtedly changed the course of her life forever. Eventually, Becky finds her way back to God, but her journey took seemingly never-ending twists and turns in favor of her demise.

As a little girl, Becky went to church faithfully and it was actually the highlight of her week. She excelled in school eventually too, even though it was because she hid behind her schoolwork. Early on Becky couldn't attend school because of an emotional and nervous condition. This condition caused her to have massive hair loss, severe tremors and all-consuming fear and anxiety. While in school one day, her teacher whispered to the classroom aide that the child was shaking too badly to even hold a pencil. Becky had no idea they were talking about her. But, next thing you know her mom, Venis, came into the classroom; the teacher told her mom that she could no longer attend class and that Becky wasn't able to keep up with the rest of the class because she was shaking so badly.

Her mother was told to get her checked out and treated before she could return. What her teachers didn't know was that behind closed doors, Becky witnessed the most horrific beatings a human could take. Her mom was the victim of domestic violence.

Venis stood 5 feet 2 inches tall and wore about 120 pounds, while Becky's step dad, on the other hand, stood 6 feet 2 inches weighing 280 pounds or more. Becky would lie in bed at night armed with weapons to assist her mom when the beatings started. She slept with knives, forks and screwdrivers every night. All Becky could think about was saving her mother from the pain and from those bloody beatings.

Although this situation was painful, nothing could have prepared the girl for this; Becky remembers it like it was yesterday; during one of the beatings somebody called the police. Thank you God, help has arrived; she thought. By this time, the family had seemingly given up on Venis for staying with a man that whipped her that way. Nobody knew that her mom stayed because she felt she had to and not because she was stupid. Aside from the beatings they had a wonderful life. The girls had most of the things they wanted and all of their needs were met, all except the need for safety and security.

Shortly after the call, two police officers arrived on the scene to find Venis covered in blood. A neighbor informed the police that Venis's husband had kicked the door in, causing the lock to fly off and bust Venis in the head. Becky and her little sister Zina stood by helplessly as the police attempted to subdue their step dad. More officers were dispatched to the scene as he beat the crap out of four officers, and eventually got away.

Confused and scared Becky wondered what she could do? Where could they go? Who could help them if the police couldn't? And why wasn't God doing something about all of this? They ended up at an aunt's house only to find their stepfather, Gary, already there when they arrived.

For years they ran, he came and they returned home. The more this happened, the less folk seem to care. The more isolated they were, the darker the clouds became. Understandably, Venis and the girls were at the mercy of Gary, the bread winner for the family. Venis was what you would call a "kept" woman and home maker, so she was always faced with the same dilemma, security in staying with the pain of the beatings. What a dilemma! Venis chose for a long time to give her girls some of the finer things in life—trips, clothes, a nice and well decorated home, all the toys two girls could play with, fine cars, jewelry— and so she stayed.

Thank you Jesus, hallelujah! The day came when she could no longer pay such a high price for the prison in which she and the girls were living. The prison of fear! However, eventually a beautiful little boy came out of the union between Gary and Venis. His name was DJ. Surely this created an even greater problem for Venis! The family's troubles were taking on a whole new meaning. If Venis and Gary weren't going to be together, what would happen to DJ? Well, put it like this, if Venis and her girls were going to have any remnants of peace, that beautiful little boy had to go. This broke mom's heart. What a choice to have to make?

In the end, DJ went to live with Gary. This was especially painful for Becky because that little boy and the love she had for him was the safest place she had known for a long time. The one good thing in her life was now gone.

Finally, after about 5 years Venis and the girls went their separate way, but the saga continued. As a result of a failed relationship, no job, the loss of her son and a lot of bad feelings Venis' life was a mess. She and the girls moved around a lot in the beginning, at times going from place to place. It was impossible to establish and or maintain any real friendships for the girls. Venis was out on her own; free at last. Rebecca and Zina watched as their mom fought hard and long to put the horrors of that old nightmare behind her, but to no avail. In order to make this work, their mom would need some money coming in, she needed her own place and she needed time to heal. Finally, all of these things happen for her and ultimately make her stronger.

With her step dad gone and DJ out of their lives, it was extremely sad. Although there were plenty of advantages to her mom being free of that relationship, there were some disadvantages too. Even at four and five years old Becky could see that sadness in her mom's eyes. Her mom cried a lot at night. What a horrible trade off! She watched as her mom went from physical abuse to emotional turmoil, sadness and depression. There was absolutely nothing that she or Zina could do.

Chapter 2

Eventually life balanced out a bit; by this time an older brother Dave had resurfaced. Rebecca believes he was in the country with a relative to ease some of the strain off of their mother of providing for all the kids during those difficult times. When Dave returned to live with them, he was a great help to the family. Now for the other brother, he was with Becky's mom's mother. So, it was Becky, Zina, Dave and Venis.

Just when it seemed to be safe to feel again, Venis decided to go out one night with a neighbor and was in a very bad car crash. As a result of this accident, she was in the hospital for nearly six months and the girls were sent to stay with family members. Of all places, Becky and Zina got stuck at Aunt Lela's house. A place that was over-crowded already without them. People were sleeping on top of one another. All Becky and Zina could think was, where was their mom and when was she coming back? Day in and day out, that's all they could think, especially at breakfast time when they had to eat powdered or canned milk. The only cereal that would cross that table was those God awful Cheerios or Rice Krispies. If their mom hadn't done anything else, she certainly made sure they ate really, really well.

To put it mildly, those poor girls were suffering and grieving, and nobody seem to care. At Aunt Lela's house you were neither seen nor heard. You got up in the morning, you ate, you sat quietly and watched the soaps all day and walked to and from the bootleg. The happiest time of the day was when their uncle came home. He would always buy the girls chocolate ice cream.

However, as if the situation wasn't bad enough, now Becky had another problem. Her teenage cousin decided to get his sexual thrills from her. Remember, Becky is only 5 at the time and this started after the second or third week there. Going to bed at night used to be a good thing because each tomorrow was hope that mom would be coming home. That changed quickly.

I think a part of her died that first night, and she knew that there was no way she would allow Zina to die like that. From that night on, Zina was placed in the back of the bed in between the mattress and the wall. Becky would pull the mattress out and slip her down onto the box spring and lay her against the wall. Becky could not for the life of her figure out what she had done in order to deserve this. This is what she thought all day and all night as she lay. Why would an almost grown man want to hurt her down there like that? Why? What was that thing he was putting between her legs? What is the stuff he squirts all over her face when he was done? Why did she have to use the dirty toilet rag to clean her face when he got done? Was she dirty, nasty, and ugly like that rag? She often wondered, when would God strike him dead?

One of the worse tragedies of all was the dirty dollar he left on the pillow after every encounter. Becky wondered if her cousin knew that he was hurting her and if so why didn't he care? Increasingly Becky worried about Zina being his next target, but refused to let that happen. She laid wake at night while her baby sister slept, watching as the footstep covered the door. Zina never understood why her sister made her sleep in the back on that hard box spring. Sometimes she even cried to sleep in the front, but Becky loved that little girl enough to say NO.

Eventually, Becky and Zina got the bad news. Their mom would not be out of the hospital for months. She had to have her spleen taken out, and the doctors said she would never walk again. For the girls this was bad, but for Becky it was the beginning of what felt like a never ending death. Too bad their real dad couldn't take them. Day in and day out these girls yearned for the love of their mother and the comforts of their home, but to no avail. The driver of the car that God awful night survived too; her face nearly got destroyed. It went through the windshield. They were coming from a cabaret and Venis's friend wrapped her car around a light pole.

This extended the playground that pervert of a cousin had established with poor Becky. He was about 17 or 18 years old at the time and smelled like urine all of the time. He still wet the bed. The misery of the pain that little girl felt every night while being taken, raped, and stripped was numbing to her already aching heart. As she recalls the blank stares at the ceiling in that small, empty, and pale room. The shadows of the trees outside the window occupied her mind while this animal took from her something that could never be replaced.

Quite naturally, those two precious girls wished there was some way their dad could rescue them, and eventually get back together with their mom. Becky secretly wished this everyday of her life. She really loved her dad and thought of him as her hero. The greatest man she had ever met. Always wondering why they were not a family like all of her other cousins' families were. They were actually the only ones who didn't have the typical family—a mom, a dad, and children all in one house. Every day that Becky remained in her aunt's house, she sank deeper into a hole that had no lights.

At some point, so long after their arrival at Aunt Lela's that Becky had lost track of time, Venis was released from the hospital. She had a long battle ahead of her, not being able to walk and all. Although it was sad to see their mom like that, using a walker and all, that was the happiest day of Becky's life! She could sleep in her own bed again. They had matching sheets, towels, and wash clothes. Thank God for grandfathers and big brothers! Those two guys took responsibility for the two girls and Venis. Maybe things would be alright after all.

Grandpa played a major role in the rejuvenation of the family. He cooked, he cleaned, he baby sat, and he nursed Venis and taught her to walk a little each day. He refused to believe his baby girl would never walk again; besides, Venis had survived all those brutal attacks in the past. She was definitely a stallion—a great woman with a big heart.

Chapter 3

Dave had to grow up and do what he had to do. He took as good of care of his mom as he could at about 9 or 10 years old. He tried to keep the girls' hair up and keep them neat and clean too. Venis really did have a lot to be proud of when it came to her son.

During this time, all Becky could think about was her mom getting better. Surely she couldn't bring herself to tell her mother that she had been a bad girl while at her aunt's house. See, by this time, in her mind all of it was her fault. Surely she had done something to cause the molestation. She never wanted to disappoint her mom and definitely not now. She could wait to tell her mom that her kootie kat hurt and to ask what that stuff was coming out of him. Needless to say, eventually these memories disappeared deeper and deeper into this poor girl's soul, almost as if it became part of who she was.

Thank goodness for Grandpa, because Venis regained her independence slowly but surely. She started out with a walker, and then she used grandpa and Dave for support and eventually started to walk on her own as they let her go. Life was starting to look better and better for the family.

Early school years for Becky and Zina were challenging still because Venis was always trying to find a better place for them to live. She wasn't going to just be satisfied with what she could get; although a lot more stable emotionally, still she struggled financially. By the time they reached John Tyler

Elementary School the girls were as happy as they had been in a long time. They had developed some meaningful and caring friendships and were eventually reunited with their other brother, Warren, who had been raised by their grandma and great grandma. The city life was new to him. He had never been out of the country. It excited him and he seemed genuinely happy to be with the family. They were finally all together under one roof.

Venis was doing it! With all of the kids in school, a stable home, some healing, and some hope, Venis became the mother of their block. Despite all that she went through and how little she had, she assisted and shared with everyone—a legacy that her family cherishes 'til this day.

By this time, Becky and Zina's real dad was more visible and saw the girls regularly. Eventually their mom met someone who appeared to adore her and they moved out of the hood. For some strange reason Venis keeps her place in the hood though she doesn't stay in it. Life couldn't be better. They were in a single family home in the suburbs with a man who has accepted all of Venis's kids as his own. He cared for them, he provided for them, he housed them and eventually, announced that he wanted to marry Venis. This was the happiest Becky had ever seen her mother, ever. Venis had lost her oldest sister to breast cancer a few years back, and was caring for two of the kids when she could. The boy came to live with them and was accepted by their new step dad Lawrence.

For the first time life was like a storybook, like a fairytale. There was a God after all. Now Becky had the kind of family that ate at the same time everyday, the kind like other people in the family had, with a mom and a dad. This was how it was suppose to be. Lawrence had been in this big gigantic house all by himself! But now the girls had their own room, each of the boys had separate rooms; they had a rec room, and a big front and back yard with a manicured lawn. This was great!

On the day they went shopping for new beds, it really felt real. Zina and Becky were so excited and they could tell that their mom was feeling a great sense of pride too. She finally felt like she and her family were out of harms way for real. That night, Venis and Lawrence tucked Becky and Zina tightly away in their new beds before leaving to go hacking. Lawrence was a cab driver part time. Although the night ended perfectly, with mom and their new dad kissing them goodnight and leaving for work, it didn't last long.

The next time the girls saw Venis she was a wreck and Lawrence wasn't with her. He had died shortly after they left the house while behind the wheel of the car. He had a heart attack right in front of Venis. This poor woman, if it weren't for bad luck, she wouldn't have any. As their mom broke the news to the family, the darkness begin to form again right then and there. What nobody other than Venis knew was that Lawrence already had a wife (though he had asked for a divorce). Before their mom could prepare them for what was to happen next, Lawrence's wife showed up demanding that they vacate immediately. Back to the hood they went.

What a way to return to the hood, same old same old. Absolutely nothing had changed; the same folk who were on the corner when they left were still on the corner when they returned. As you can imagine, this was especially hard for this family because they had never been that happy before and couldn't imagine being that happy again. Thank God they still had that one bedroom apartment to return to! Venis was gifted that way, almost as if she knew. But the girls didn't even get to keep the beds! This was devastating to the family and time was the only thing that could help them.

Chapter 4

Going back to school helped take the kids' minds off the situation and gave Venis a chance to properly grieve during the day. Venis loved the kids enough to be strong for them, after all, they had witnessed more than their fair share of heartache. She was very committed to keeping the children as free from worry and fear as she could be. Unfortunately, eventually marijuana creeps into the picture, along with a beer or two. This really seemed to uplift her and act as a coping strategy.

One day Venis seemed to be living again and her and the kids were back into the swing of the game of life once again. They were definitely soldiers; nothing could keep them down. This was a very, very intimate and close knit family. They ate together, they played together, they did their homework together, and they hurt together too. Home was a safe haven for them, especially for Becky. Having both her brothers and a nice comfortable home was good for her while she dealt with the horrors of her own pain.

School was a place where Becky excelled; she stood head and shoulders above her peers academically. She seemed to be a born leader, even without trying. But soon that was challenged too. Becky made a split decision one day that could have changed her life forever, but not so because of her age. On that faithful day her actions were a cry for help, but nobody picked up on it. They just put her down, yelled at her, and told her how awful what she had done was.

Becky decided to hook school with some friends at lunch time and eat at the carryout. But, before going to the carryout her classmate who was treating had to go home and get some money, so off to her house they went. While there, Becky came up with this urge to make some of the girls feel uncomfortable, like she'd felt so often. She locked two of them in the closet and demanded that they kiss each other on the mouth or they couldn't come out. This was terrible for the two kids. They were begging to get out of that dark, hot and stuffy closet, but to no avail. Becky did not let up until she heard enough smooching and kissing to satisfy her need for somebody else to hurt like her.

By the time they made it back to school there was complete silence among the gang; it was about five or six of them that day. What nobody knew was that the money they went to the carryout with was that girl's mother's rent money, and that all hell was gonna break loose when her mom found out they had been in her house. Not to mention her daughter being forced to perform despicable acts of indecency. By the time that girl's mom was finished Becky was at the police station in the interrogation room. Venis was furious and totally embarrassed, but she stood by Becky anyway. Fortunately for Rebecca, she had a great reputation up until that point and the fact that she was only 9 years old led to all charges being dropped. However, she was forbidden to speak to either of those girls again.

That was the beginning of a lonely time for Becky because many parents, teachers, students, and friends turned their noses up at her; but she made it.

She continued to excel in school and was able to refrain from that type of behavior again. By the time she made it to fourth grade, she knew intuitively that she should never hurt anyone that way again; this made all the difference in the world in how she dealt with her pain of rape and molestation from that point on. Although it didn't turn out well for her in the end, she was able to minimize the harm she caused others. After all, at 9 she still couldn't understand that the stuff her cousin did to her while her mom was ill wasn't her fault. She could still feel that nasty, thick, sticky, stinky stuff on her face every now and then. What had she done to cause it? Why didn't she tell somebody? Surely that made it her fault. If she did tell, who would believe her and what would they think of her? Was she nasty? Was she really going to hell? Was God really going to strike her dead? Was she a bad girl and more importantly, was she as ugly as that semen made her face feel?

Becky often wondered what she could do to escape these feelings and thoughts. She was never, ever free from the bondage of that time in her life. If only somebody realized that her behavior toward her friends was a sign of an even deeper problem. Good girls don't just get up one morning and do things like that. Some how Becky yearned to be a good girl, she wanted to be a good role model for Zina. Even when she didn't think of herself, she cared about little Zina. That was always her shadow. She had to be strong and focused for her. Zina wasn't as mature as Becky and therefore she took responsibility for her and her welfare when Venis wasn't around.

To make matters worse, Becky was outside playing two days before her ninth birthday when she had to use the bathroom. She ran inside and realized she was bleeding. She didn't know why, but didn't tell anybody for fear of not being able to finish playing. Later she didn't bother because she didn't know what to say. Rebecca felt the same that day as she did when she needed to tell her mom about her kooty-cat hurting. Thank God Venis came in the bathroom after her and noticed the blood on the seat. She said, "oh my God, my baby!" That child had no idea why her mom would react that way. Of course her life changed that day forever. She now had to be careful not to let anybody else in the house find out her secret; menstruating at eight years old. She was ashamed and embarrassed. She found herself afraid to run outside with that thing down there, afraid it might fall out. She remembered how she feared her wig coming off when she went down the sliding board. Becky had to wear a wig to school back when all her hair used to fall out. It took some time for those shots in her head to work. Her fears came true one day, her hair piece fell off and those kids laughed her off the playground. Venis was so hurt when she found out, but did what any mother would do and encouraged her baby to go back to school and eventually get back on that sliding board.

Who amongst you can imagine what this child felt like, going to bed with hair and waking up with it on the pillow? Not only was she black, darker than everyone else in the house, but now she was bald too. What a monster to have to live with every day and every night.

The horrors of this girl's reality began to take shape though she tried hard to be a good girl. Soon the one good thing outside of her home began to be detrimental. There was a neighborhood church pickup for anybody wanting to go to church. Mount Zion was the name of the church. Many of the kids from K Street went, including Becky and Zina. Church seemed to be just what the doctor ordered for Becky, but what she didn't know was that rapist and child molesters were there too. The predators dwelled among them. Zina and Becky watched as other girls played church. They shouted and pretended to be in the spirit all of the time. They shouted until folks had to sit them down. They fell out as soon as the preacher laid hands on them and for Zina and Becky this was so funny. But without failure, after the service those same girls went and smoked cigarettes, drank beer and even had sex with men.

Doomed to be Nothing, Destined to be Something

Chapter 5

Thank God for Becky's sake she never fell into that trap. A sign that God watched over her even then, because even at ten and eleven years old the girl was built like a Coke bottle. The men were coming at her and her age didn't seem to bother them, not one bit. But Becky and Zina sang for the Lord, traveled with the church, were baptized in the ocean up in New Jersey, went to bible study during the week, went to prayer service during the week and any other service. If the doors of the church were opened and they could be there, they were. Rebecca remembers times when she and Zina had to catch the metro bus and walk through some pretty rough territories to get home, but God was with them.

The church thing didn't last for Rebecca though, because the overseer of the church married a man who felt it was ok to lay hands on Becky in ways not ordained by the Lord. The only thing Becky knew to do was run like hell for her life. That was it for church for Becky for a while. Nobody ever knew why, except her and the Lord.

By now the girl felt like, "what's the use?" and began to act on some of her fleshly thoughts and feelings. She began playing boys chase the girls a lot. She recalls enjoying some boys' nasty, sweaty, filthy hands on her. She just needed some type of an escape from her horrible reality, if only for a moment. All Becky could think was that there was something awfully wrong with her for all of these men to keep coming to her like that. She must be doing something.

If only someone could have ministered a word to this child, she could have known that rape is never about the victim. Sexual abuse is about power and immorality; it's never about the child. She just needed to know that she wasn't a bad girl, and that God loved her still. This would have made all the difference in the world to her.

Becky declared herself a child in darkness but afraid of the light too. Despite all these things, Zina seemed to still look up to Rebecca and she always knew that her sister would protect her. Venis really did raise the girls to be close, and to stick together in good and bad times. It made all the difference later on in their lives.

Rebecca talks openly today about those shots she had to endure in her skull for about 2 years in order to sustain her nerves and to regrow her hair again. She still remembers what it was like to see the tears well up in her mom's eyes each time the doctors put Becky in that straight jacket to administer the injections into the skull. She took all she could take and eventually asked that her mom not make her do it anymore. She told her mom that she would rather be bald than go through that another day. Venis honored her daughter's wishes; although it was hard to see her baby bald and feel in her heart of hearts it was because of all the drama to which she had been exposed. Becky had a chronic nervous disorder.

Because God is good, he allowed Rebecca to get her hair back and live as normal a life as possible after that. She was able to be sustained just because God said so, not because of any shots, or any other drug. No more shots, no more rapes, no more violence against her mom, and no more moving around, all because of the grace and mercy of the Lord.

Maybe God cared about Becky after all, she thought. Maybe she wasn't as nasty, dirty, and ugly as she'd always felt. The thought that she was just as good as any other little girl was a foreign language to Rebecca and it had eluded her all of her life. In a room full of her peers, she felt alone. Either she was too ugly, too black, too big and tall, and at times with bald spots all over her head. This was not a pretty picture, and as a child you can't began to fathom how or why this was so. If God was so good, why did he let this happen to me, is what Rebecca often thought. He must be punishing her; it had to be her fault.

Soon Becky also had to deal with the changes associated with getting older on top of her already enormous since of despair and low self worth. Hormonal changes, coupled with all of the other things with which she was dealing was challenging to say the least. After six grade graduation, the peer pressure was on. Boys were coming from everywhere and it appeared Becky was in demand. What a relief it was to be wanted and desired by her peers!

It was during this time that Rebecca started to take second looks in the mirror, and one day she realized that her big eyes had a nice slant to them, and that although she was dark, she didn't have any marks on her face. She also began to see the value in her big behind and large breasts; the ones that were always seen as huge and in the way by Becky. She got a lot of attention, even if at times it was negative. It was liberating for Becky to see boys do double takes, cars stop, and horns to blow as she walked. What a welcomed change for a girl so unsure and so full of self hatred! Thank goodness Venis had told her girls about the one thing guys wanted and how they would tell you anything to get into your pants.

Chapter 6

While most of Rebecca's peers were hooking school and jumping in and out of cars, she remained faithful to her education and future. She did well her first year in junior high school, but she struggled to do so. To go from feeling like the ugly duckling to a swan in demand was an overwhelming change; one that she wasn't sure what to do with. It actually seemed easier to be ugly, awkward, and nasty. That way she didn't really expect much and she didn't stand the risk of her brother reminding her on a good day that she was just too darn black. Coming out of the comfort zone was difficult for her, but she did it. It was so nice to hear folks ask if she was a model and if not she should consider it. There had to be a God after all. But obviously the enemy had set up shop in this young girls mind long before God was ever really really established there.

By this time in her life, Becky is allowed to talk to boys on the phone; it's her eighth grade year. She found herself head over heels for a young man, who proved to be her worst nightmare in the end. If only she had known, if only she could have gone to Venis. Too make a long story short, after talking to him for an extended period of time on the phone, he gave Becky the ultimatum of coming to him or him going somewhere else. Becky really didn't want to go to him, but she surely didn't want him going elsewhere either. What should she do, she thought that night? She couldn't sleep. The next day she left school at lunch time, but not before deciding she would be back by next period.

The agreement was that they would not really have sex that day because Becky feared it would hurt; he would only open her a little each time until it didn't hurt anymore. Well, after about two or three minutes, she couldn't take it anymore. He said ok, but next time they would really do it. Becky left and went to the bus stop to get back to school. Whoa, is all she thought when she made it back in time. Not only had she kept her guy from going elsewhere, but she also made it back in time for fourth period. Maybe now she could sleep!

The pressure subsided and she felt like she had established herself with the love of her life and was off limits to all other boys. She remained committed to school and to her dream of one day becoming a supermodel. She enjoyed being on the runway; she and her favorite cousin modeled for many department stores back then. She loved the feeling of power and acceptance she felt on the runway. When people were screaming and clapping for her, it made all the difference in the world to her broken esteem. She was really coming into herself.

Becky had also been blessed with the pleasure of a friendship that was very special to her. This girl, one of her neighbors gave Becky the courage to persevere in spite of all of the whoring, partying, and hanging out that went on in the neighborhood at that time. Although her best friend Sinai had a baby by age 14,

Becky looked up to her because she was working and going to school. Venis did not approve of the relationship and tried everything she could to keep them apart. Even though Rebecca wasn't sure what it was at the time, there was something about Sinai that made her feel comfortable and safe; taken care of. This was especially attractive because Becky spent her time taking care of Zina and Venis early on.

Doomed to be Nothing, Destined to be Something

Chapter 7

Venis had met another man by this time. He had swept her off her feet and married her. He was one of the people on that corner of K Street about which Becky talked. Venis said this man made her feel like nobody else ever did and that she was going to give him a chance and encouraged him to come in from off that corner. He did and she got his hair cut. From there he moved up the social and economic ladder. Eventually, he moved them all from the hood into the townhouse where Becky met Sinai.

Venis was so happy she had her own husband. He accepted all of the children as his own and never once complained. Surprisingly, Venis got pregnant and had a baby boy named Jodi. He became the light of Becky's life, almost like DJ. She embraced that little fellow like he was hers. But soon Venis noticed Becky acting strangely. She seemed to be eating strangely, over sleeping, and not being active. Her diet began to consist of Oodles of Noodles, macaroni and cheese, Pepsi, and junk food. No matter what Venis cooked, that seemed to be all that the girl wanted. So Venis demanded Becky to go to the doctor. Becky didn't see why, because in her mind she hadn't actually had sex yet. All he did that day was open her up a little bit; in her mind Venis was going to feel stupid when she found out that Becky hadn't done anything and wasn't pregnant.

Boy was Becky wrong; she was pregnant and in big trouble. Venis, Becky, and Auntie Dee went to the doctor that day. Thank God for her aunt because her mother would have beaten the crap out of her if it were not for Dee. After careful consideration, Venis decided that the baby was going to be aborted because her daughter had a great future ahead of her, and Venis wasn't ready to be a grandmother. This was so very embarrassing and humiliating to Venis. Her daddy was speechless and could only remind Becky that she had lied to him about having a boyfriend. What a mess that one decision had made in her life and the lives of her family!

Rebecca would have given anything to not be in that situation. After all, she had just started to feel worthy of the good things in life. She had begun to feel a sense of value. By that time, she knew that she was smart, she felt attractive, and possessed a talent for fashion and hair, and she was beautifully built. All of which was being threatened by this pregnancy. And the father, he did just what her mother said he would do, ran like hell. Once his parents found out that Becky was pregnant, he was enlisted in the military and she was told not to be calling or looking for him either. What a mess! Eventually his sorry butt called, filling Becky's head with all sorts of false hopes, which lead her to believe he would help care for the baby.

Becky didn't want to get rid of the baby and felt her only hope of keeping it was to run away. Well, wouldn't you know that after 4 months of carrying the baby, the father sent her a letter and card with a pregnant goat on it advising her to take care of the baby; if it was his! This was devastating to this young girl, and she really did feel all alone. She didn't know what to do or to whom to turn, so she dealt with it just as she had the molestation. She didn't want anyone to know. This guy had turned on her and there was nothing she could do about it. It was too far along for her to have an abortion, even if she wanted to at this point. Stuck and out of options, she carried the baby to term and began her life as a single parent. Needless to say, she flunked out of school despite trying hard to make it, while Sinai went all the way through and graduated. Tragedy seemed to be the season for this family because Venis had just had an unplanned pregnancy, Becky was pregnant, her oldest brother was in and out of jail, and now their family was being evicted.

    The U.S. Marshals were moving all of their belongings outside of the house. Thankfully, Venis had gotten a U Haul truck to make it look like they were just moving to passers by. They left their beautiful spacious townhouse and moved into an old, tiny, rundown box around the corner. Amazingly, by the time Becky's baby was born that place actually felt like home. Venis had a gift of turning nothing into something, and making any house into a home.

    Now that the baby had come, instead of looking forward to getting her drivers license, going to prom, graduation, and becoming a supermodel, all she had to look forward to was dirty diapers, sleepless nights, making bottles, and all of the millions of other responsibilities that come with being a mother. This child thought she had the worst luck imaginable. She was a magnet for trouble, and this time it had definitely changed her relationship with her mother. Venis took that one act of ignorance on her daughter's part personally and it hurt her deeply.

Becky spent her time trying to repair their relationship by working harder than the others, cooking, cleaning, and caring for her younger siblings in any ways that she could. This was her way of letting her mom know that she loved her and that she was sorry for letting her down. Her father was also very, very disappointed because he had very high hopes for her. He also seemed to take it personal. It was too bad for Becky because now she was in the scariest situation a girl could be in without the emotional and spiritual support of her parents. It was just too difficult for them at the time. She knew they loved her but she just didn't feel it.

Chapter 8

Becky presses her way with the baby, and tries to go to night school. The family has moved again and this time to an even greater place of despair. Of all places the projects, they ended up in Kenilworth. That was the scariest place in the world for the kids to reside. It was a lot cheaper to live there than it was to live in that old tiny house that had become their home. But now the decision to move there proved disastrous. The area introduced them to all kinds of drugs, sex, violence, and threatened the productivity of the entire family. Everybody was caught up over there, a bunch of parties all the time. Some times the whole building where they lived was partying. Doors opened, curtains flying out the windows, and borrowing bread and sugar was the happening thing around there.

Of all the obstacles thus far in Becky's family's life, this was the deadliest one. The oldest son Dave fell into the trap immediately, followed slowly by their mom, then Becky, and then Warren; the other son who had always excelled, fell victim to a level of violence you wouldn't even wish on your worst enemy. That was the straw that broke the camel's back. Venis packed her stuff and got her kids the hell out of there. She actually asked if they could go and stay with her husband who had left them to their dysfunction a while back. Lucky for them, he said yes. Another horrible move, from one hell to another is where they went.

The space was limited in his apartment and tempers flared all the time. Becky found herself working hard to make her mom happy and trying to keep up the house. Venis hated a dirty house and raised all kind of sand about it. The best thing to do when she got that way was to be quiet and get to working. It was tough, but they made it work.

The crime and drugs were phenomenal, it ruled and anything that got in the way of making that money had to go. Soon Rebecca's family was on drugs. They spent all of their money on drugs, and they became divided. The one person in the family who remained drug free was little Zina, but she ended up in the psych ward at children's hospital because of all of the dysfunction in the house. She became suicidal in all of the madness. Soon it became very obvious that this poor family was in deep trouble and that without help they would all fall through the cracks.

Eventually Venis's marriage began to crumble, and the family values that once held them down rapidly began to go up in flames with the cocaine they smoked. One thing that didn't seem to make any sense was how mean and detached Becky's mom seemed to be; she was pushing all of the kids away from her. She began to tell folks to get the hell out and to find their own places to stay. She didn't seem to have the same embrace she used to have on good days. It was very odd to her children.

The drama continued to unfold as they were eaten alive by the effects of cocaine. By now Rebecca was lost. Zina was out of the hospital and with their dad and his wife, but didn't want to be. The people she had always looked up to were simultaneously letting her down. She and Venis began to experience some of the same feelings Becky and Venis had encountered some years earlier. Becky and Zina stuck together a lot through all of this. If their mom put Becky out, Zina would often look out for her and the baby. If Zina got put out, Becky did the same. Sometimes they would leave together.

The other thing Rebecca had going for her at this time was a close bond with her older brother; the one from the country. He was always there for her and didn't seem to mind what others thought she was. He seemed to have an admiration for her, like the one DJ had had. Although at times there was nothing he could do to help Becky for fear of being thrown out too, he always offered moral support.

One day everything finally made sense to Becky. Venis and the girls were at home, paddling around the house. Rebecca entered the bathroom without knocking and caught her mother off guard; she saw one of the most horrific sights she had ever seen. Her mom's breast was corroded; it was dark, bruised, hard, swollen, disfigured, and purple. It took Becky's breath away, but she could see she needed to be strong for her mom. Venis was relieved that someone found out about her dreadful secret; she had breast cancer. She had refused treatment for fear that it would cause the cancer to spread, and thus it got worse and she was dying.

All of the things she was doing were explained when she said she was just trying to prepare them for her death and make sure they would be able to survive without her. "Zina! Zina!" is all that Becky could yell. The two girls embraced their mom and gave back to her what she had always given to them, before the drugs anyway. Rebecca convinced Venis to go to the hospital to be checked out. She went and they suggested that the breast be removed immediately. Off it went.

After the surgery, and for the first time in a long time, Venis seemed to breathe again. She was at ease. She could talk to her children and look at them again. This experience rocked their world, but only made them stronger as a family. All that Venis had put into her family manifested in those moments. Venis had done an awesome job, even despite falling victim to drugs and all of its dysfunction. Now homeless, ill, and afraid, Venis and her family tried to put the pieces of their lives back together. They were scattered here, there, and everywhere. Venis's recovery proved to be a lot more challenging than ever expected. She could not be left alone. She was afraid to go to sleep and would only sit up in her bed for fear of falling to sleep and not waking up.

Eventually, the fear of her near death got the best of Venis and she turned back to cocaine; come to find out, she began her use of cocaine in the first place to cope with the pain. Rebecca discovered during her mother's return to drugs that she was again with child: and in her mind at the worst time possible. In her family, whenever a baby was born, someone died; so she felt the baby was going to replace her mom—a thought that was too much for her to bear. This was a reality that she did not welcome with open arms. Becky too turned to drugs with an even greater pursuit than before. Soon she went on a rampage and almost killed herself. Mind you, Becky has a young child too that has to live through the horrors of her mom and grandmother looking like they are dying due to the drug use. Thank God for Aunties; Zina watched out for that baby as if it were hers and eventually turned to her dad and stepmother for help with the baby. As much as Becky loved Toni, she couldn't care for her properly.

On one of the visits to the hospital to sit with her mom, Becky was asked to do something against her better judgment despite being on drugs. Her mom asked her to go to the house and bring back the drugs and paraphernalia she was using prior to being readmitted to the hospital. Although she knew that it was wrong, Becky could not tell her dying mother no. She left the hospital during a snow blizzard; it was the blizzard of 1987. She left on foot. That was the darkest day of her life and the last time she saw her mom alive.

After leaving the hospital, a man saw Becky walking in a dress and some boots in the snow and offered her a ride out of pity. She agreed to give him money to take her to her mom's house and so he did. While there, her mom called and asked her to not only bring the drugs at the house, but to also make a stop over in the projects of paradise on the strip to buy more. Becky advised the man that she needed to make one more stop, and off to paradise they went.

Going over into paradise projects was a scary thing, nothing but gang violence, sex, money, and death reined over there. Courageously she went though and did what she was told to do. Venis seemed to always have a very high admiration for this girl's strength and courage. She knew that if anyone would make this happen for her it would be Becky. When Becky and the man pulled up to where he found her, she began to sob and he asked what was wrong. She revealed to this stranger that she was about to take the drugs from her mom's house, as well as the hundreds of dollars in drugs she had purchased over in paradise back to the hospital for her dying mother. He looked her in the eye and said, "You will never live it down if she expires while using the drugs that you gave her," and advised her not to do it.

Chapter 9

Becky was only 19 years old at the time, addicted, pregnant, and scared to death about her future without her mommy. Rebecca left with that man, with all those drugs, and about $500 of Venis' cash. She was taken to a safe place to think about what she was going to do. She knew Venis would be furious, and when the family found out, there would be hell for her to pay. After 4 or 5 days of hiding and using drugs, Becky decided to go home and clean up in order to face her mom and family the next day. She had to tell everyone the truth about her messing up and about what their mom had asked her to do as well.

Another sign to Becky that God watched over her was when a friend hit the number and gave Becky all of the money she had spent of her moms. Too bad for Rebecca that she didn't go home when she said she would. The folks around her at the time were only preying on her and her obvious grief; she laid those lottery tickets down for one minute and they were never seen again. That's what junkies do; they were like vultures.

Home she went, which at that time happen to be with a cousin in Landover, Maryland. She talked with her cousin Connie about what was going on. Connie encouraged her and gave her a warm embrace. She took a bath, and prepared for her visit to face her mom in the morning. Early the next morning the phone rang. It was Zina and Becky could hear Connie ask, "What's wrong? What's wrong?" and Zina saying, "I want my sister!" In that moment Becky knew her mother was gone.

She left for the hospital immediately to face the family; it was bad enough she had to face them about the drugs and money situation but now after her mom's death. Everyone was very angry and upset with Becky. They only knew Venis's side of the story. Talk about hard times. This was devastating to Becky because just when she needed her siblings the most, they rejected her deeply. They were hurt that she would just run off with all that money; they had no idea about all of the drugs she was to bring back. The only thing they seemed to know was that she ran off with all of Venis's money and demanded to have it all back.

Of course they went ahead with funeral arrangements, which Becky had nothing to do with; she and baby Toni stayed away and hitched a ride to the funeral because she missed the wake due to getting wasted. As much as she wanted to stop partying, she couldn't. Her need to escape won over her need to say goodbye to her mother. Now she really was the bad guy; not only did she run off with her mother's money but she couldn't even show up for the wake. This was a place of utter despair for Becky, but she pressed her way the next day to make it to the funeral.

Her family was as cold as ice and rightfully so, given what they had been told. Also, they had no idea how all of this was affecting Becky. Soon she had to tell them that Venis had ordered her to bring those drugs back, and that she had to go out in a blizzard while pregnant to get them. She said she was sorry but it took some time for the family to embrace her again. So she proceeded to self destruct at an even greater pace.

While at home after the burial, trying to move on, Rebecca began to bleed. Her cousin called the ambulance and off to the hospital she went. What happened next to this child was unbelievable to say the least. She was on the exam table about a minute when a white woman came in complaining of labor pains. She was told to get down, get dressed, and that her baby was fine. As much as Becky objected, it did no good.

When her cab arrived at the hospital to take her home, she stepped in and flooded it with blood, clots and clots just running out. Scared out of his mind, the cab driver yelled for help. They came out with a stretcher and wheeled Becky to the operating room. While rolling down the hall, Becky signed consent forms. Briefly, she saw her baby girl as they rushed her off to be taken via helicopter to Children's hospital. After 2 days of being in the hospital, a doctor came in and asked furiously why Becky was in this ward with the new mothers? Rebecca yelled that it was because she was a new mother, but got no response. All she could hear from her room was a lot screaming and shouting.

Doomed to be Nothing, Destined to be Something

Soon she was moved to another floor and shortly after a social worker and a doctor came in to advise her that her daughter died enroute to the other hospital. This hit Becky like a ton of bricks; not only was her mother gone, but now her baby too! There was nothing that could help her to make sense of this. She frantically called her stepmother to tell her about the death of the baby. Her step mom advise that she have the body released in order to have a proper memorial, to help bring some closure. When this grieving young mother asked to have her baby's body released the doctor and social worker told her that the baby was being used for experimental purposes and that she had been cut up and placed in jars; part of the consent forms she had signed ignorantly! At that moment, she could have easily lost her mind, but only for the grace of God she didn't. It had to be God and him alone. She could never have been prepared for something that horrific and over the top, but it was actually happening and to her astonishment it wasn't a nightmare or dream. She obviously broke down at this news and became hysterical; security was called and she was escorted off the property.

She left the hospital that day as numb as a human could get. No drug in the world could fix that. She smoked and smoked, but found no relief. The darkness she once knew in her early childhood had returned, only darker. And this time it came without her mom to make it better or brighter. She tried countless times to get her life in order but couldn't. Soon she found herself in places she never thought she would be, with people she never dreamed she'd be with. Now she was homeless, her mom was gone, her baby was dead, and she was cut off from her family and out there in the big old world all on her own; a sure setup for disaster, given her history.

Doomed to be Nothing, Destined to be Something

Chapter 10

One day she met a man by the name of Felix who seemed to take an enormous interest in her and Toni. Everyday as she walked her child to school he followed closely in his cab making small talk. After much persistence he was granted a date and things went pretty well. Seemingly, this was the one good thing that happen aside from being able to stay with an old friend of Venis's. She and Toni had their own room there; finally a place to call home again. However, soon the novelty wore off because the young man never wanted to go home, and eventually began to stalk Becky. Although she wasn't suppose to have overnight guess, she allowed him to stay over in order to prove she was faithful to him at night. She didn't want him to have fits of jealousy and peek through the windows at night from the neighbor's yard. Soon his overnight stays became a problem because while they hid the car at night and he hid under the bed, someone eventually walked in while they were all asleep and found him there.

Becky was warned to get rid of that guy because he was crazy and was going to hurt her. This soap opera drama went on long after she left that house. He and Becky began to use drugs. Becky's step dad took her to rehab after her mother's death and she was off drugs since that experience. Now back on it again, Toni was sent to live with her grandparents. The family was very tired of the drama of Rebecca and this guy, and backed off; sounds familiar, doesn't it? They eventually got a place of their own. They had slept in the car a lot of nights and at the YMCA. Although he beat her when ever he felt like it, that relationship was the only thing she had that seem like hers. The beatings were vicious, and he blamed it on the fact that she used drugs. Yet each time Becky stopped, he found a reason to beat her anyway and then buy her more drugs. For a young girl full of grief and confusion, this was both challenging and overwhelming.

They moved to North Hampton; the suburbs in Maryland. It was so beautiful there, but the affects of feeling lonely and imprisoned started to take hold of Becky. She was literally locked in the house everyday with no way out, even if a fire had broken out. She had no contact with the outside world other than him. Soon she reached out for her family and they availed themselves again. When the isolation got the best of her and the streets began calling her name, she started jumping out the window. When she returned she would tell the maintenance man that she locked her keys in the house so he would let her back in. After doing this for a while, one day she got stuck and going home wasn't an option because she couldn't wait until she got home to get high. This time she started smoking as soon as she got it and never made it home.

From that moment on she was on the run; she was ducking and dodging Felix. She knew he would be furious and possibly whip her butt when he saw her. People in the neighborhood began to tell Becky that he was looking for her, offering to by rocks for anyone that lead him to her. He began to stake out the hood in order to catch her. Fortunately for her, days went by, no Becky. She eventually called him to say she was sorry, and to tell him that she was hanging out with a friend. Of course he wanted, rather demanded, to know who. He wanted her name, her address, and anything else she could offer to make her story credible.

Becky returned home only to be treated more like a prisoner than before. This time she had to strip at the door. Her clothes were tied up and trashed! She was asked to bathe in bleach and disinfect for being around those nasty, filthy bums in DC. He said she probably had bugs and some more stuff. She was very hurt to say the least, but feared getting beat. After a few days went by, things seem to be back to normal. Felix brought home ingredients for spaghetti the night before, so Becky decided to make that for dinner. While cooking, she got a phone call from her oldest brother Dave. Felix was so over protective and territorial that it angered him when she gave anyone else some time or attention. He came in, looked her up and down, and went on to the back. She softly advised him that it was her brother in order to appease him. She said something he didn't agree with so he snatched the phone out of the wall, smacked her, laughed in her face, and ran into the bathroom. This made her furious and caused a very, very destructive reaction. She began to take the bathroom door down. She could not believe what had just happened. She had been home all day, cleaning, washing clothes, and was fixing his favorite meal.

At some point, he came out to deter her from kicking the door down. He made the God awful mistake of touching her again and she broke free and threw that whole pot of steaming hot spaghetti sauce on him. He was running around in there, screaming and hollering for dear life. He begged her to do something, but she couldn't. He went running out of the house butt naked, yelling, "Help! Somebody help me!" When he returned, he was accompanied by three or four police officers with guns. Upon entering the apartment, Becky was told to get down on the floor. Their guns were drawn and the officers were yelling at her. At some point, she realized she was going to be locked up, and thus began to ask why when he was beating her for no reason and had been for more than a year. When she said that, the officers turned the guns on Felix, ordering him to the floor. To Becky, that was a welcomed change. She was tired of him making her have sex when she didn't want to, plus he was so large it was inhumane. It was like surgery, and she just couldn't take it.

Chapter 11

He was taken off to jail, and advised not to return to the apartment for 30 days when he gets out, so that Becky could find a new place to stay. That didn't last though; as soon as he was out, he started calling, crying, and begging. Before long he was back in the house. She told him that in order for him to come back, he would have to stop checking her underwear all of the time, and she didn't want to sit in the middle of the seat while riding in the cab to prevent her from looking at other guys from the side mirror. She wanted his solemn promise that he wouldn't beat her anymore for going down an aisle at the supermarket that had a man in it. He agreed to all of these things and more. He said he would even stop forcing her to have sex, and that did it. Back to the apartment he came. She felt bad by this time and tried to forgive herself for getting him locked up, even though he was the one who called the police.

The changes didn't last a week. While riding in the car, she sat on the passenger side and not in the middle as agreed. Well, he began slapping her while crossing Benning Road in rush hour traffic. This caught her totally off guard and she either snapped or lost her mind, because she took an umbrella and began beating the mess out of that man. When it was over she was driving the cab because he had left on foot trying to escape the vicious beating. Soon she caught up to him, gave him the vehicle, and got out. Where she was going was anybody's guess.

She ended up over there where all of the bums lived in DC, according to Felix. She wandered those streets, getting loaded, and eventually met a guy who was very, very nice. They partied together whenever he wasn't working and eventually one thing lead to another and they got together. He insisted she not go back to Felix, because he feared he would hurt Rebecca. The trouble with that was she knew he wouldn't go away that easily. She was always looking over her shoulders and one day her worst nightmare came true; Felix pulled up on her while with this new guy Jerry. They were just walking down the street to the store and he jumped out of his car like the jump outs. He asked what the hell she was doing and because of the response he got from Jerry, he got back in the car as fast as he came out.

This was a good sign; maybe he would leave her alone after all. Nope, it was simply wishful thinking. Her fears began to be outweighed with the feelings of acceptance and freedom that she felt. Becky began trying to get her belongings from Felix, but to no avail. He threatened to trash them if she didn't come home. She stood her ground even though he had all that she owned; she would not allow him to own her soul anymore. She started over with the clothes on her back. She tried once again to get her life going in the right direction with Jerry's support.

Becky found it necessary to tell Jerry about her child and how much she missed being a mom. He encouraged her to do what she had to do in order to be reunited and offered to do what he could to help.

Things didn't go as smoothly as they planned because, while Becky tried hard to leave the partying behind her, everybody in the house was indulging all day long and at times all night. Jerry didn't understand the effects of him and his friends doing this around her. She managed to hold on, get two jobs, save her money, eventually get her child back, and in the meantime she cared for a niece and nephew.

It felt good to mother again, but she began to be overwhelmed when her own child returned. Becky turned to a sibling for help, and he took one of the kids to relieve her. Becky also soon realized she needed to get a place away from there with the kids. She talked to Jerry and he agreed, but nothing happened. She decided to go out on her own, though she had never done so before. Miraculously, she got a one bedroom apartment not far from there in a secure building. Upon getting the news, Jerry was visibly shaken and could only offer his apologies for not taking her seriously enough. He asked if he could get one more chance at getting them out of that place where they stayed and she reluctantly said okay. In a matter of 2 months, he came home and asked her to take a ride with him; they stopped the car, got out, went up the steps, and he gave her the key and said welcome home honey. It was a three bedroom single family home.

This was the best thing that had happened to her in a long time. She thought she was dreaming. She was elated and felt so optimistic about her life, and couldn't wait to tell the kids. Now she could quit one of her jobs and do some other things she'd always wanted to do, like learn to drive, get her GED, and decorate her new home. In no time the house was beautifully decorated, neatly stocked with everything they needed and lots of what they wanted too. Too bad for the family that material things don't equal happiness, and they don't work late in the midnight hour when your gut is flipping and your soul aches from the injuries of yesterday. She gave it her best, but often times found her self lost, uncertain, and afraid. Most days she would just ignore it and keep doing the right thing, but this could only carry her so far. If only she knew that man, the one they called God. With her enthusiasm being challenged daily, and her gratitude fading with boredom, she fail victim to the ailments of fear and inferiority.

Without God she could do nothing and she knew this, but could not find her way back to him. She tried countless times, by going to church faithfully. She was actually attending on a regular basis when she relapsed. She says it was like yesterday, she fed the family, cleaned up, and decided to get some movies and popcorn for Toni and Jerry. She would be gone no more than 15 or 20 minutes at the most. For some strange reason, her car had a mind of it's own that day. The next thing you know, she was back home, no movies and acting stranger than ever. Toni was very, very perplexed by this and reluctantly asked, "Mommy, did you do it again, did you?" This was the worse day of that poor child's life. She was finally reunited with her mom only to be faced with this.

Chapter 12

Nobody could have imagined the roller coaster ride this family would take. Needless to say, all the pain of the past still haunted this now grown woman and until she faced it and her fears surrounding it; she'd never, ever truly be free. Of course Jerry and Toni were devastated by this and just tried to be there for each other. They seemed to think it was just an awful mistake and hoped and prayed it wouldn't last long, and that she could get a handle on it before it completely took over. This was at the worst time possible for Toni, just when she was beginning to feel safe and all. You could see the pain in Jerry's eyes as he watched the enemy steal his best friend right from under his nose and there was absolutely nothing he could do.

Soon he too fail victim to the very thing from which he tried to save Becky. Now Toni was in trouble for real. What was she going to do? The journey that Becky took from that point on was very necessary in order for her to receive God with an open heart and a made up mind. Too bad her family didn't understand that and at times rejected her and talked about her badly. Nevertheless, they did what they could to protect Becky and Toni as best they could. Becky found the courage to face what she'd done and tried to clean it up to the best of her ability. What a relief this was for the entire family, although short lived.

With things seemingly back to normal, Becky attended the outpatient aftercare program, and even enrolled in college courses at the University of the

District of Columbia. She was doing quite well and was obviously very proud of herself. Her grades were good, she was feeling good, and most of all she had the support of her family behind her. The joy Becky felt inside could be compared to nothing she'd ever felt before, so what would make her turn back? This was the million dollar question everyone wanted to know the answer to.

It was time for a family vacation, and off to Missouri they went. They drove across country and enjoyed each and every moment of it. When they got to Kansas City in the area where Jerry's sister lived, Becky began to thank God for a safe trip. Out of no where a car approached at a high rate of speed; hitting them head on. Becky was driving at the time, and all she could think of was that they were going to die. Amazingly, nobody got hurt because she was able to shift the wheel in a way that caused damage to the side of the car and avoided a head on collision.

They were greeted with open arms when they arrived at Martha's house, the friendliest country folks you'd ever want to meet. Finally, after all those years of being with Jerry she got to meet his family. The trip went well until Becky began to feel really bad, almost as if she had the flu or something. She didn't seem to want anything to eat either, highly unusual for her greedy tail.

Soon it was time to hit the road and make their way back to Prince Georges County, Maryland. They said their goodbyes and off they went. They were happy to be back at home in their own beds. Life couldn't be better, except that ill feeling continued for Becky, so she decided maybe she should make an appointment with her doctor.

Meanwhile her girlfriend wanted to hang out a while, so off to the club they went. While there, Becky saw a cousin whom she beat the mess out of for disrespecting her and Venis while Venis was dying in the hospital. Becky was actually staying with this girl at the time her mom was in the hospital and she made the mistake of saying, "F your mother," to Becky. Why did she say that? Becky lost it and beat the hell out of that girl; she had not spoken to her since.

When her cousin spotted her she reluctantly came over with open arms, so Becky did so in return. They set a date for the following weekend to celebrate Becky's birthday together. Becky had no idea what was in store for her. Friday came and Becky left to go pick her cousin up. Mind you, all week Becky kept hearing about this bomb gift she was going to receive; talk about an ambush, the devil really knows how to do it! She was so excited, Becky loved surprises. Well, the first sign of trouble should have been the Gallon of Remy Martin, but Becky thought, "Oh, okay." No problem, because a drink wouldn't really hurt her. The problem with that was the enemy used alcohol to take down her defenses in order to have his way.

After a long, sweaty party, Becky was ready to go home. The problem was that her cousin wasn't done with her yet. She asked if they could make a stop, so they did. Eventually, Jerry called to check on Becky. When he realized they had been drinking, he advised her cousin should go home in the morning and that Becky should just come home. When they got there Becky got some pajamas for her cousin and went upstairs to get comfortable. She was excited to have her cousin back in her life, and really wasn't ready to go to bed. When she went back to the basement to check on her cousin and chat; she never expected to see a big white cloud of smoke and a huge flame. Her cousin had actually purchased two eight balls on that stop they made.

Becky wondered why her cousin couldn't see that she was clean and didn't smoke or drink anymore as she proceeded down the stairs. By the time she reached the bottom she had become hypnotized by the flame, the white ball of smoke, and the smell and asked for some. This was a night she would not live down for a long, long time.

Up and down the road Becky went from PG County to Charles County getting high. She hid it for a while from her family, although Jerry knew. Soon he barred the cousin from their home and then Becky began to spend more time down the road with her instead of at home. This was particularly bad because she was still in school and poor Toni did not have a clue. Jerry kept her dirty little secret as long as he could, but felt he needed to do something. Whenever Becky was home Jerry and Toni waited on her hand and foot because all she could seem to do without drugs was lay around. Soon they came to the conclusion that she should have kept her doctor's appointment.

    Off to the doctor she went, only to find out that while in Missouri the ailment she had was morning sickness and not the flu. Devastated, she left the office with tears running down her face, feeling doomed to be nothing one more time. However, Jerry was elated and told everyone. Jerry did not seem to understand why this was upsetting her; to him, it was the best news he could hope for; something that would permanently tie him to Becky. It was almost as if he'd forgotten how her life began to deteriorate in the first place, and all of the pain surrounding giving birth up until this point. For a moment Becky wondered who the hell she had been talking to all those years. Finally, it became evident that she and Jerry had two very, very different views about what was happening.

    The plan was for all of the partying to stop, for her to eat right, get her rest, and be as stress free as possible. Jerry agreed to do everything in his power to show her that her life wouldn't take the same tragic turn in carrying his child. He was a darling and very supportive emotionally; he tried to avail himself as much as he knew how. For Rebecca, it was not enough to calm her fears and to shut off the nightmare that was taking place in her head and heart. Soon the bondage to the fear got the best of her and she stopped trying. Soon she was on her way back to Charles County, and she never bothered to tell her cousin that she was pregnant.

Doomed to be Nothing, Destined to be Something

Chapter 13

Before long, Jerry spilled the beans on her to her brother, and DJ was furious with Becky. DJ was living with Becky at the time because of a hardship in his life. This posed the biggest challenge ever to a great relationship. They were the best of friends, and now she was going to lose him again. But not even the threat of that could help her get it together. Surely she was in deep, deep trouble. None of the going to church seemed to help either. Nothing seemed to be reaching her, nothing. Soon she began to be afraid for herself because she knew the places she went, she shouldn't, and the things she was doing, she shouldn't. The only thing that could save her was God, no amount of family ties or love was going to do it.

By the grace of God she managed to keep the kids fed and a roof over their heads during all of the madness. Somehow Jerry made it to work everyday and brought home the bacon. He was very, very committed to the relationship although it appeared to be in shambles. As you can imagine, life took on an entirely different meaning in a once beautiful and peaceful house. Soon Becky was unable to stop partying for even a day and therefore she put her fetus at risk. Although she wanted to do the right thing, she just couldn't say no; not even to save her or the unborn baby's life. She was just a complete mess up, or so everyone thought.

Giving birth to that baby girl of hers was life changing to say the least. She was captivated by that little girl. Even though this was an unplanned pregnancy and even an unwanted pregnancy; she falls head over heels in love with that child. She wanted nothing to do with that old lifestyle and she made that known to all who would listen. Jerry knew to get rid of any and everything that would remind her of the old times. Too bad that by the time she was ready to start over, Jerry was all in and had absolutely no plans to stop. This was a very, very painful time for Rebecca because she had to watch her baby fight through the shakes and God knows what else because of her bad decisions. The baby was in the hospital for over a month after birth; it was oh so sad because she was so small. The doctors didn't feel she would ever be normal, but Becky refused to embrace information like that about her beautiful baby.

    Before it was all over she had the minister come and pray over her child and she believed with all her heart that victory was hers in the situation and that no weapon formed against her or her child would prosper. Now all that she had to do was try to get Jerry to give up on the old lifestyle before it sucked her back in, leaving her two kids to fight for themselves. No amount of talking, begging, or pleading seemed to curve Jerry's appetite for the drugs and alcohol. Becky always lost when she tried to come between him and them. She found herself looking for him when it was time to go to the hospital to feed the baby; she was breast feeding.

    She began going alone and facing the horrors of her behavior on her baby alone. This seemed to be the only thing that got her attention; she was the one who had started this destructive behavior. Too bad feeling terrible didn't last longer; soon after Tyra was released from the hospital the partying started again. One night while funning, Becky realized there was something very, very wrong with the baby. She screamed for Jerry and they went to the hospital. When they arrived, the doctors advised them that Tyra was in need of a blood transfusion. With her judgment impaired, Becky had to make a decision, fearfully because of the AIDS and HIV epidemic. She turned to the same faith she had when the doctors first told her that her baby wouldn't be normal, and gave consent for the procedure with confidence.

Somehow in all of this Becky recognized that even in her sin, God still loved her, and continued to show her favor. Another scare was just not enough to cause them to change. Now Becky couldn't breast feed anymore, otherwise the baby would be exposed all over again. She often wondered how she was going to take care of her kids, knowing that she couldn't even care for herself. What a space to be in when you have two beautiful children that you absolutely adore, but hate yourself for what you've become! Though she didn't know how, she just knew that she was going to make it out. There had to be more to life than this, and she wanted some of it.

The day came when she gave Jerry his ultimatum; get a divorce or she was taking the kids and leaving. Too bad for Rebecca her man didn't take her seriously, because she found the divorce papers he'd claimed to have filed months ago in a file cabinet.

This devastated her; she was actually mentally and emotionally planning to be married. She had even asked her stepmother to find a hall for the reception. She felt like such a fool; he had been playing her all the while. Nothing he said could sooth her, one more time she felt like a loser, but this time with 2 kids instead of one. What was she going to do? Carry out the threat, with no money, nowhere to go, and really nobody to turn to? She felt too unworthy to turn to God, and too embarrassed to turn to family. Trapped in a role she desperately wanted out of, all she ever wanted to do was be a productive member of society, somebody others trusted and respected.

Up until this point all she had felt like was a sex object, a toy and playground, a whipping post, and door mat on which others wiped their feet. With a mentality like that it's no wonder she ended up in such a dark hole. If only she could see past her circumstances and believe God for her and her family. Hurt and pain seemed to be suffocating her, she couldn't breathe. Locked behind the doors of her broken home with no sun light, no fresh air, and by this time no more visitors either. Darkness was all around her, and change looked very unlikely. Yet there was something about the possibility of folks taking advantage of her kids that gave her the drive to just keep trying, because if she couldn't protect them, who would? Her children would eventually lead her back to God. When Rebecca didn't love her self enough to look to the hills from where her help comes from, her love for her kids kept her and carried her.

Chapter 14

Thank God Tyra was okay and back to normal. The baby's illness was a great opportunity to turn things around, but for Jerry and Becky it proved to be a lot harder than they ever expected. They suffered a great deal more before desperation and despair whipped their behinds and humiliated them even further. After some time of living like an animal, Rebecca only felt comfortable coming out at night, too afraid somebody might see her. Almost like a vampire, what a way to live! Feeling hurt and betrayed by Jerry regarding intentions for her, she moved out of the bedroom into the basement with the understanding that there was to be no more sex, none!

She never put her foot down like this before, ever. He was furious, almost as if she belonged to him and he had a right to her. Well he didn't cooperate with her and was always in her space. She asked that he leave her alone and just go back upstairs where he would normally be, but to no avail. Soon he began sitting and taunting her. Too bad for him, he did it to her while she was as high as a kite one day and she threw a meat cleaver and hit him smack dead in the face, knocking out some of his teeth. She watched as his mouth filled with blood and his teeth began to fall. Of course the look in his eyes communicated that he was going to beat the living day lights out of her, so she ran as fast as she could. She ran until she couldn't run anymore.

She hid for a few days, and eventually went back into the house. There was blood everywhere. Mind you, when she ran, she left the kids. They were home when she returned but there was no sign of Jerry. What she didn't know was that her family was taking him to take out a warrant for her arrest. Reality had set in and Becky was full of remorse for what she had done. It was too bad Jerry didn't take kindly to the space she tried to put between them. Now the sheriff was looking for her with a warrant for her arrest. She was scared out of her mind, but not enough to do something different. She began to frighten herself at this point; what was it going to take? Assaulting Jerry should have been a wake up call, but not for Becky.

Rebecca waited for days for his return, but there was no sign of Jerry. Soon she got the nerve to ask her family members where they had taken Jerry, because Toni told her when she came home that they had picked him up. She wanted to know where her man was, but nobody seemed to know or even cared for that matter. Fear began to sit in because she had the kids, the bills were due, her cravings were off the chart and she had no money whatsoever. What in the world was she going to do? Nobody wanted anything to do with her. Filled with sadness and despair, she locked herself in the house and emotionally deteriorated. The only thing that could bring her out of it was some mind altering substance, anything.

She couldn't bear to face her own reality anymore, the mess that she had made of her life. She was too ashamed and embarrassed to even turn to her favorite Aunt Dee for help. She even referred to herself as a monster at times. She said she felt like something or someone invaded her body and spirit and took over. She couldn't do right even though she desperately wanted to. She could not function with or without something to pick her up. She was doomed no matter what. The very thing that gave her an escape and a vacation from her dark soul was failing her too. If she couldn't stop, surely she would end up killing herself or someone else.

She was very, very aggressive toward others in the end. Her fear that folks would try to take advantage of her or her children now that Jerry was obviously gone and out of the picture caused her to be overly aggressive. Toni would often open her window and watch as if watching a movie while Becky assaulted or physically removed someone from their house. It was hard to believe Becky could be so forceful given how very tiny she was.

One day a neighbor came by and he obviously wanted something from Becky that she wasn't willing to give, making her very uncomfortable. She asked him over and over again to leave, but to no avail. Rebecca knew in that moment that she had to do something or surely she was going to be victimized by this man. She thought quickly and opened up the basement door while neighbors were outside; she began pulling this man and screaming for him to get out of her house. She pulled and pulled until he fell out of the chair and then got up. Seemingly, he was going to hit her but the neighbors were outside. Eventually she got him outside, but then he got into her unlocked car that was parked in the driveway. She was very irritated but it was better and safer than him being in the house with her, Tyra and Toni, so she left him alone. Becky had a strong vibe that she was going to be raped, assaulted or even worse.

Chapter 15

She went on with her day, buried in that basement, isolated from the world. Rhonda, a friend of Becky's at the time knocked on the door, just checking to see what Becky was up to. They decided to run to the store and to make a pickup. When they returned, the block Becky lived on was swamped with police cars, ambulances, and fire trucks. She thought to herself, "oh my God, my kids." She had to leave her car at the corner and run to her house, there were road blocks everywhere. When she got there, Toni and Tyra were fine once they saw that their mom was alright. Now that Becky knew all was well at home, she wondered what was going on. What she found out almost caused her to lose her mind. She was in a state of shock. The guy, a neighbor, who she had escorted out of her house about an hour before went into his house and asked his dad for $10 to get some drugs. When his dad said no, he blew his head off with a shot gun; the same guy was begging Becky to give him drugs for sex!

"Oh my God," was all she could say and think because God let her know intuitively earlier that she was in danger, and that is the only reason she thought to get that man out of her house! A sure sign to her that God was still fighting on her behalf and that she hadn't fallen totally from his good graces. She just didn't know how to turn things around all by herself; she felt so alone and so afraid. Soon she found out Jerry had left her and the children all alone to move to Missouri and was devastated. Becky had to find a way to go on. All she could think about was how and why this was all happening to her. It began to feel like a nightmare from which she desperately wanted to wake up from.

Strung out, alone, hopeless and afraid she had to pick up the pieces of her broken life and clean up what she had messed up. She did not have a clue how she was going to achieve this. She did know that God would be a great place to start. She found herself many, many nights sitting and partying with tears rolling down her face as the gospel played. Sick and twisted is what it sounds like, however, God does what he wants when he wants. Seeds were being planted even in her storm. Life began to be more despair than pleasure and she didn't want to live at times. She was afraid to live, but afraid of dying too. She wished it secretly though, but always thought of her kids. What a sad existence for those poor children?

If the cycle was going to be broken, Becky was going to have to do it; if she was going to give her children or her grandchildren any chance at all of a productive life, the buck had to stop there with her. This was not the legacy she wanted to leave behind.

Thank God for tragedy, because soon death was all around Rebecca and her children. People running through the back yard in the middle of the night, gunfire everywhere, police officers being shot and killed, and folks she just had conversations with being accused of the murder. This freaked this woman out. All she knew was that God would have to intervene in some way. But she could not seem to pull herself out of the rut. Soon she realized Jerry wasn't coming back and decided she was going to have to do something in order to survive in that big house by herself with the kids. Thank God for brothers; DJ was grown by this time and had reestablished his relationship with Becky. He was her savior many days and her enabler too. However, it didn't take long for him to get as far away from her as possible too. The pain of watching his sister go through that was a great burden to him.

When DJ left, Becky thought, so what now? On one of her trips to get some drugs to get high, she ran into a guy who she absolutely despised; when he saw her, he would often cross the street. But guess what! Soon after this particular meeting he came to her door with a lot of money and they got high. They became road dogs or partners. Was she now to despise herself too? They got along just great; he was actually a great guy that had simply lost his way and was just trying to survive too. For the first time in a long time Becky didn't feel alone anymore. This guy made sure she and the kids had whatever they needed and a lot of what they wanted. They were like the best of friends; she was everything he lacked and he was everything she lacked.

Doomed to be Nothing, Destined to be Something

Chapter 16

They made a decision to become intimate and the relationship changed drastically after that, in the sense of the emotions that were involved. It was not business as usual anymore. They began clocking each other and stuff like that. Anyway, on one of his trips to do whatever it was he did to get the money and all the other stuff he got, Rebecca heard lots of sirens. She didn't think anything of it and just lied down and went to sleep. Only to wake up hours later to find out he had been arrested. Her heart was so heavy at that moment. She was right back to square one again.

With nothing and nobody, she had to go on. When reality set in, she knew he wasn't coming home for a long time. He had been caught coming out of the window of a private residence. He had tripped a silent alarm and the dogs were sent in by the police with the house surrounded. Those K-9 dogs devoured him. This saddened her deeply because he had been so good to her and her children and there was nothing she could do for him. It seemed like God was removing everything and everyone from her life.

Tragedy seemed to always be around Becky but it never struck her, only those around her. Was she really highly favored, did God still really love and keep her through all of this? Wow, maybe that's why when the man attempted to abduct her, the car door opened, even though it was obviously locked and had been rigged not to open. The door opened, she jumped out, he ran over her legs and attempted to reverse the car and do it again, and she somehow got up fast enough to escape the additional torture. How she was able to run like hell after that is anybody's guess. She ran like Forest Gump, despite being injured. Too bad she ran straight past her house to the strip to cop.

It was probably for the best anyway that her partner got locked up and all. A few weeks before, Becky was going up the street to get a beer and had the weirdest experience. She told Toni to listen out for the baby, who was asleep, and to eat some popcorn and watch a movie, and that she would be right back. Off to the store she went, but she never made it. On her way up the hill, a van pulled up beside her and they snatched her; she was taken to another location where she was presented with lots and lots of mug shots. While driving to the secluded location they just kept asking her, "where is he? Where is he? Your boyfriend, we know he's been in and out of your house. He killed the police officer that was murdered in his driveway the other night." Becky was shook for real when they said that because, if they were right, she would be darned if she did, and darned if she didn't. God was she glad when she saw the mug shot of the guys for whom they were really looking for. It wasn't him after all. After being held and questioned for hours, she was let go. They took her to a dark street and dropped her off. It had been the feds.

She needed more than a beer at that point. She'd never been so happy to see her kids in her life. Wow, what if those people weren't police? What would have happened to her, she thought? It was like something in the movies. A dark van pulls up, doors open, and in she was pulled. Surely it could have gone the other way just as easily. This reminded her of the time she went to a friend for money and after catching a cab with her last dollar to go to get the money, they didn't even open the door for her. Not only was this disappointing, but she didn't have a way home either. Forced to walk, she started up Southern Avenue when a driver, who seemed like a nice guy, stopped and offered to give her a lift. While riding in the car, she struck up a conversation with him and began talking about her children and how much they meant to her and how she really, really wanted to be a better mother. Then, all of a sudden he pulled the car over and said, "Get out!" She was startled and said, "What, did I do something wrong? Please, it's dark out here, please don't put me out." While reaching for his gun; He said, "I picked you up to rape and kill you, but your talk of your children touch my heart. Most of the women out here don't even care that they have children, let alone speak about them. So go home to your children." If this wasn't a true example of God's love for her, she didn't know what else it could be.

Doomed to be Nothing, Destined to be Something

Chapter 17

Back at home with the children, she searched her heart for what she was going to do; she knew it was only a matter of time before something horrific happened to her. What would happen to her babies? She couldn't be selfish and cowardly any longer. God was going to have to do something, send somebody who understood her way. Either that or death; she already died a spiritual death a thousand times. More and more she yearned to get out, but still didn't really know how. What in the world was it going to take to get her moving in the right direction again? Surely the grace of God covered her and had been for a long, long time; she knew soon her chances were going to run out.

Talk about being afraid; talk about feeling hopeless and at a loss. She yearned to see Venis again, if only just one more time. Her mommy always knew what to do, even in the worst of situations or she at least made them easier to bear. She returned home and laid in a fetal position that night with the hope that God could or would reach down and do something, anything with her; take her out! Just kill her or let her die in her sleep or something. Either that or set her free, deliver her from the hell she had built in running away from her childhood pains. She ached to be normal, to just be able to get up, be interested in something other than one more, just one more, chasing a feeling she would never get again. She had so many other things she wanted to focus on but couldn't because of the compulsion and the obsession to escape again and again. She was in desperate need of help, and she needed it fast.

Over the next couple of months, she purposed not to use anything over and over again, to stay true to herself, and to try to spend time with her children. A day or two would go by but that seemed to be as long as she could stomach her own self and her life without drugs. She just couldn't do it. Soon the lights and the water were off. She tried to get help from the state, but that would take a while. She stayed in the house as long as she could, but eventually had to go to a shelter. While there, she got a job working at night while a young lady in the shelter kept the children for her. She worked until 2 a.m. and had to walk the darkest, spookiest walk home to get back to the shelter. She was walking under bridges with no lights on eastern avenue, dark roads with warehouses and nothing moving other than the rats, crack heads and junkies. How fearful, but she had to do what she had to do. Amazingly, while there she didn't drink or use anything; a great example for her to try to follow once she was back at home.

Soon she had the money to get all of her utilities turned back on, so she went back to the house and the same old nonsense she had left behind while at the shelter. It was all waiting for her when she got back. Nobody seemed to care that she and the children were somewhat happy. She was glowing like crazy, but not for long. She once again fell into her surroundings and her environment. Eventually, family members started to pressure her to go away to get refocused. She made many attempts but could never seem to follow through. They became discouraged and then just gave up because they knew she wouldn't do anything about the way she was living until she really, really got tired.

People in the neighborhood were dropping like flies. The murder rate around there was so high. She was afraid to even sit in front of a window for fear of a stray bullet. That was no way to live, and certainly not with children. Thank God for the Department of Social Services; the vehicle God used to bring her out of captivity, bondage, and despair. It was hard, but she did it; it took a lot of dedicated people to see her through the misery and mess she had made of her life, but she made it. In order to do it she had to face some ugly, ugly facts and she had to confront some very, very painful memories. She could no longer hide in a bottle or a bag.

It proved to be harder than she ever imagined. Paralyzing fear gripped this woman and sent her running for real now in search of anything that wouldn't allow her to feel. The Department had there hands full with this one, and eventually had to call in a higher authority. The social workers asked that their supervisor accompany them on visits to Becky's house. Surely this was a text book case, something you would have had to see in order to believe. She was a pack of bones, but very, very intelligent and strong willed even in that shape. She was most honest with them, sometimes too honest. They weren't ready for that. Rebecca made it out though and only God could have pulled her out from under all of that mess, finally she agreed to go to treatment. On her way to face the reality she ran from for so long, they made a stop. Oh the devil is a liar!

Chapter 18

This could only have happened to Rebecca. The social worker advised her that time was limited, and that while she got some personal items for her and the kids, Becky should go to a near by McDonald's and sit and eat. The trouble was days before Becky had asked them to hold a few hundred bucks for her. Well, wouldn't you know, they gave it to her and left them at McDonald's. She was supposed to sit there with her child, eat and wait to be picked up. The trouble was she had that money and drug dealers were in plain site. Well, she did what anybody in that situation would do, she started craving. She got a bright idea; she was going to leave her child in the high chair eating her happy meal, while she ran across the street to cop. She went for the door, but it wouldn't open. It opened for everyone but her. She did not have the physical strength to open it. And it was in that moment; she looked back at her beautiful child and simply said, "Oh my God, I really do have a problem."

That was her first real surrender to just how helpless she was. Glory be to God, she sat there and waited for the social worker to return and took her journey to get some help. Becky recalls entering the treatment center as the scariest day of her life. But, she entered that sacred place in the mountains where everybody looked as if they needed a friend or a hug. The staff was very, very understanding and professional. They gave her hope for the first time and she felt as if somebody really, really understood her and that just maybe she could be helped after all. This was probably the biggest decision she would ever make in her life.

To many, the deck was stacked against Rebecca because at the time, she only went for her children; she didn't think enough of herself to do it. But God uses whomever he wants, when he wants. Her children were the vehicle that God used to get her out of harms way. It was only a matter of time before one of those bullets would have been meant for her or one of those women found naked and bound up down on Southern Avenue would have been her. But there she sat in a room full of strangers with no clue how these people would be able to help someone like her.

Soon questions started arising about why or how she was there. She heard it all, and most people were sent by courts or parole officers. Rebecca was only there for the love of her children, which they strongly advised wouldn't work. She was ridiculed by her counselors the whole time she was there and told she wasn't going to make it, if she was doing it for the children; but God. What they didn't know was that the love this mother had for her children was strong enough to prevail over her obsession to use drugs. While there, she was praised for being an awesome mother; she was told how beautiful and pretty she was, how intelligent she was, and how much her group members believed in her. This was major for her, considering what the counselors were telling her about coming for the kids. She was told after her graduation ceremony that she was not ready to go, but she wanted to get back to check on Toni, who she had left with a friend and with whom she hadn't had any contact in a month. It was recommended that she stay for at least 18 months, but there was no way that Becky could leave Toni to someone else to love for that long, she just wasn't comfortable with that!

Before she left the treatment center, she was given an assignment to write her eulogy as if she died today. Honestly speaking, what others would think and feel about her? It bought tears to her eyes to do this. The things others would say about her in the midst of her children tore her heart to pieces, but it was all true. However, the second part of the assignment was to write the obituary as she would have it from that day forward and it brought joy to her soul. She was instructed to hang this on her room door. She had to bury the person in the first obituary each day before leaving her room and speak this new person into existence in the latter eulogy. This did wonders for her, even as a very reluctant woman. Eventually, she buried her old self and there were no more tears, only the joy and enthusiasm of walking into her destiny of her new life. She was being transformed right before her peers and her child.

She decided to leave after a month and return home. On the day that she left she was advised not to go back to the house that she left, but to go to a shelter with her kids. At first, she was appalled, thinking, I'm not going to no shelter. So, off she went up the road to go home. But God intervened when the fear of losing all she had acquired while there frightened her and she asked the driver if he had a phone. She called back to the treatment center and asked if the shelter was still available and they said yes. They went to the shelter instead.

While there, she encountered many obstacles and strong forces that seemed to be working against her, but no matter what, she held on to her commitment to her kids and self. God was changing this woman in spite of herself. He didn't seem to need her permission in order to take her to the next level. Soon she was starting a mentoring program for other women struggling with using drugs and in abusive relationships. This was very instrumental in her recovery because she began to feel like a productive member of society and her community. Women were looking up to her, looking to her for guidance and supervision. Oh how the tables can turn, and for all those who counted her out; good God almighty!

Chapter 19

There was obvious work for Rebecca to do and God wasn't finished with her yet, oh but God. She had 90 days to try and make something happen in her life and then her time was up at the shelter. As frightening as this was, she pushed and pushed to get some things in place for her and the children. They were poor as all out doors but had everything they needed. For Becky this wasn't going to be easy because the moment she decided she wanted to live right, Toni decided she didn't.

All hell broke loose in Becky's life again. She held on and tied a knot in the rope and whichever way the wind blew she went with it with the understanding that no matter what, she was not going to let go or give up. Soon Rebecca was coming home and finding evidence that people were not only hanging out in her house, but using drugs as well. By this time she is out of the shelter and living in her own apartment for the first time in her life. It was truly miraculous the way that it happened. The social worker who was assigned to her and her family from over at the shelter was truly a demonic spirit and definitely a challenge for a woman new in recovery, to put it nicely. She did nothing to assist Rebecca, and every door that opened for her the worker would intervene and prevent her from receiving a lot of the resources the other women were getting; women who were still using and being irresponsible. All Becky could think when it hurt so badly or she couldn't even push out a prayer, was hold on to God's unchanging hand and a song by Yolanda Adams, The battle is not yours, it's the Lord's.

When her 90 days were up at the shelter, she asked for an extension but was denied, of course, by the social worker. With nowhere to go, she began packing her things, not sure what to do or where to go. The director of the shelter, who had watched all of the obstacles placed before Rebecca, interceded on her behalf. He pulled the company vehicle up to the door and told her to put her things in the car and off to a hotel they went. He told her not to worry and that he would be back for her in a few days; he must have paid the tab, because Becky had not. Somehow, she took comfort in his words and did not fret. After a couple of days he returned and took Rebecca to the same complex where the shelter was and gave her keys to a fully furnished apartment in her name with the rent paid for 3 months. She was in complete shock, because this same complex turned her down because she had no job, no credit history and little income. God truly does what he wants, and it really ain't over until God says so.

Now on her own, she is head of household, in recovery, a single parent, and has to deal with a teenage runaway. With many sleepless nights, she worried about where her child was and if she was okay or not. She often feared in her gut that some man was taking advantage of her daughter. On nights when she could sleep she would wake up to go to the bathroom only to find Toni gone and the door unlocked. Soon she began encountering problems with thugs in the neighborhood because the moment she found out they had any interest at all in her child she stepped straight up to them and let them know to get the hell away from her and her child, often placing herself in harms way to send a clear message. This battle went on for a very, very long time and eventually she was able to establish the kind of foundation that allowed her to go on in spite of what her child was doing.

She was in recovery and she liked it. She learned to trust God and to trust the evidence of her new life. She still had to be there for the baby. In the good book it says that a child will lead; it came to a time when her little baby had to lead her. She remembers it like it was yesterday; she came home and saw obvious signs that Toni had been in the house. She was sneaking in and out of the house while Becky was gone during the day, instead of being in school. She saw signs of marijuana smoking and blunts in the trash and this really triggered something in Becky. She decided shortly there after to just go get something to ease the pain. Mind you, her baby never wanted to walk when she went out. She was lazy and would stay home with Toni. On this particular day, she looked at her mom and said, "Mommy, I'm going to walk. Can I go, can I go?" She took her and she did just what she said she was going to do; she didn't whine or complain, as she normally would. On the way to get high she said, "Hey mommy, just pay your rent and when I be a woman, I'll pay your rent." Not realizing they are no longer in the shelter, she said, "Lets just go to the office ma." This got Becky's attention because what did this child know about paying rent at 2 1/2 years old? The youngster had grown accustomed to them going to the office at the shelter, whenever Becky had a problem.

She knew in that moment that God used her baby to save her from that old misery to which she was so accustomed. Well, she made it through it just fine and kept on keeping on and eventually realized her children were blessings and not burdens. Her whole perspective on her life was changed that day, forever. She began to see that her trials were making her stronger; she was going through the fire and it was defining and purifying her from all of the ugliness of the pass. She was beginning to walk into self and out of the shackles of rape, molestation, drugs, domestic violence, low self-worth, guilt, shame, embarrassment and into forgiveness and love for self.

Chapter 20

Soon Jerry came back to visit her and spent time with them. He was so very, very proud of her and offered to buy her a house in the Midwest if she would just come back to him. As tempting as it sounded, she knew that if she was ever going to do anything for herself she needed to stay and struggle to get ahead; for her, it was now or never. No more hand outs or free rides! She wanted to stand for something and shoot for the stars. That is exactly what she did and boy was she glad she did. She found out some wonderful things about herself that all those bad feelings had buried.

After a long bout in aftercare, Becky's graduation day from the program was approaching; she would be on her own, nobody else to tell her what to do. She had officially been rehabilitated and was fully capable of living life on her terms. This was the scariest thing she had faced clean and sober, but she embraced it with her whole heart and walked into her destiny. Having her family rally around her during this time made all the difference in the world to her. She had made them all so very, very proud. Coming out of aftercare was the beginning of a new era in her life. Now what was she going to do, she thought.

Dealing with Toni and all of her nonsense, the baby, and her own recovery and issues was very overwhelming for her at times. She began to experience the kind of fear that paralyzed her. She began to feel inferior as a result of not being able to provide for the children the way she desired and felt they deserved. Seeing her daughter wear the same pants over and over again was very humiliating to her. Thank God she knew and believed in a very small way that joy was coming in the morning and that trouble doesn't last always. This kept her going when she really wanted to give up. Looking into the big, bright eyes of her little girl gave her the strength of an ox. She always inspired her to do the right thing when the going got tough. It also was good having Jerry back with the family, and to have his love and support again. They enjoyed their time together but soon he was off to the airport, and gone again. He was not giving up on the idea that she and the kids would relocate to the Midwest with him. As hard as life was for Becky on any given day, she was willing to stick with it and stay, to pray until something happened, to ride it out with the hope of discovering just who she was and what she was made of.

Becky knew she was going to have to get a job soon just to make ends meet. This was particularly hard on the family because it left Toni vulnerable to the thugs in the hood, and the baby missed her mom terribly. Becky felt guilty each time she left the house to go to work, but did what she had to do to provide the basics for her children. Soon she began to feel the sadness of her help being gone again, and the pressure to perform under enormous responsibility as a mother, as a newcomer in the program, and as an employee and a person. Some nights she lay in bed and could not sleep to save her life. All she could think about was the horrors of her life, the murders she witnessed, the rapes, the pain of using, the lost time that she could never get back, and the torn relationship between her and her precious daughter. God this scared her and sometimes she didn't have any hope that she could fix it or that she deserved for God to fix it either.

Despite all the hardship, she didn't use any mood-altering drugs and stayed her course. Thank God for the gospel because she was in the part of town where drugs were all around her and she lived far out from the rest of her family. She had no friends on this side of town, no car, and not many options. She often used music to minister to her to move from despair and depression into gratitude and grace. Doing the right thing didn't always feel good; it wasn't always attractive either. Folks all around her were doing what they wanted to do, not practicing any principles, yet seemingly happy as could be. Somehow this didn't seem fair to her, but she had to be careful not to glamorize the lifestyle she used to live and never forget the pain and embarrassment of it all. Yes Lord, she needed to always play her tape all the way through to stay grateful.

Much of what she was going through made using drugs look better and this scared her because with using, she knew what was going to happen. The journey she was on left much to be desired, lots of uncertainty and an overwhelming amount of fear. Her faith was all she had, faith in the recovery process; faith that God would do for her what he had done for countless others, and a small amount of faith in herself. Becky had discovered some pretty disturbing news about her life; she realized that just because she was clean and living a new life, not everyone would or could accept or embrace her. She found out with some, her past would always be used against her, and with others, she was easier to deal with when she was using drugs. It began to feel like those she counted on the most really couldn't celebrate her or lift her up.

The hurt, the disappointment, the pain, the anger, and the resentment ran too deep. Oh my God, how was she going to get through one of the most painful and difficult moments of her adult life without the support of her closest loved ones? Lord, what was she going to do? She was always bombarded with crazy overwhelming thoughts that produced a great deal of anxiety and panic. Rebecca knew that she was going to sink or swim with or without certain people, so she decided to swim, swim, and swim! She jumped into her new life with everything she had and vowed to see this thing through until the end.

Working, attending the outpatient rehab program, being a mother and head of the household took its toll on her at times. There were days she desperately wanted to give up and throw in the towel. This woman was very inexperienced at dealing with life without an outlet or escape. She was terrified on the inside but well put together on the outside. She often described her feelings as the little girl in a dark, long hallway, without windows or doors. She often felt like the boogie man was following her and she would never be free of him, regardless of what she did. Somewhere along the way, she began to see a light at the end of the hallway. As a result, she hung in there long enough to see the miracle of her future unfold.

Wow! Oh my goodness, how time had flown! Rebecca was celebrating one whole year of abstinence. She would soon be celebrating one year of being in her apartment—a major accomplishment for the girl who had never been on her own and responsible for her own well-being. As if God hadn't already done enough and as if the rewards of staying clean couldn't get any better than what she had already experienced, she recounts some very precious moments on her journey to freedom and self actualization. There was the time when all she had was a black and white TV, no bigger than a window pane, and received a new 32 inch colored TV. Then there was the time when she received a $500 gift certificate for Toys R Us during a time when she had only three shirts for her baby, three blankets, and a very small amount of formula and diapers. These were very significant moments for Becky because she could feel the presence of God with every act of kindness.

Doomed to be Nothing, Destined to be Something

Chapter 21

Here comes the kicker. She was about to graduate from the rehabilitation program. She spent almost 18 months of her life there and was deemed able and available for life on its own terms by her superiors and her peers. It was an honor to complete something for once in her life. It was an achievement that she would never forget. Broken, battered, belittled, and beaten by life when she began, and she now had a new lease on life. Now she wondered what life would be like without her peers and counselors telling her what to do all the time, how to do it, and so forth? She often asked her self what she was going to do and to whom she could turn to talk about it. She really didn't know how to live without all the support and involvement of the family she had acquired as a result of being in the 18-month program. They really had become her new life and her family. They did what some members of her real family were not able to do. Now it was all gone, just like that. This brought on an anxiety she had never known, a panic that was overwhelming, and a fear beyond any prayer that she had ever prayed. Am I really ready, is what she often thought during the days leading up to her graduation. But, boy did her siblings support her. They showed up and showed out; it was so beautiful that all she could do is cry. It was a long, overdue acknowledgement of her hard work and dedication and also the grace of God at work in her life.

Folks began to trust her again, they began valuing her opinion, and they started to rely on her again. She was really being reunited with her sister and brothers! It wasn't a dream after all. It was really happening, and she needed to find a way to handle such goodness because she was not used to the stability and productivity of living this new life. She was much more acquainted with pain, suffering, degradation, sadness, guilt, shame, remorse, and low self-worth. At some point, it was even no self-worth. Finally, she was ready to go out into the real world and show them what she was made of.

Questions took over her thoughts. Where should she start? What should she do? Was she really ready? Was she worthy of all the rewards her new life offered? And most of all, will she be able to stay clean? All she knew was that she was going to give it her best shot. If God could deliver her from the pit of hell, than surely he would strengthen her to deal with her new life.

This was actually the first time in this woman's life she ever even considered being good enough, capable and able, Godly and spiritual, beautiful and wonderfully made, and a host of other feelings once foreign to her. Things have begun to happen all around her, blessings from everywhere. She was so overwhelmed with the goodness of the Lord that sometimes she could only think negatively to the point where she almost missed the enjoyment of the blessing. If she wasn't careful she would sabotage her own destiny for the fear of trying and failing. But to God be the glory, she had heard enough on her journey to deal with that too. She advises the scripture, "I can do all things through Christ who strengthens me," is what carried her during those most destructive thoughts of sabotage. She began to amaze her self because she was beginning to do things that were once unheard of in her and not because she wouldn't, but because she couldn't. She realized that God had really created in her a new creature.

Becky realized she was blessed and highly favored by God and she just couldn't figure out why, especially since he allowed so many horrible things to happen to her in her younger life. The thing that always came to mind was the vicious molestation she experienced at 5 years old. Who would have ever thought she could rise above the ugliness of that—all the fumes of his semen on her beautiful, dark face? God is awesome. He is able to do what he wants to do and is gracious and merciful. If for no other reason than for her to have compassion for other people, be understanding and less judgmental, and be enormously caring, God allowed her pain of the past in order to predestine her future. She was a born leader and really didn't know how she could have evolved to such a state without the help of a loving and caring God.

As she began to evolve into the lady she was always suppose to be, she found out she was most talented in writing. She entered into a computer class at a local, non-profit neighborhood organization to make herself more marketable; because though she was evolving spiritually, socially and economically she was at a stand still educationally. She decided to hit the pavement running. Rebecca recalls the unsafe and insecure feelings she once knew when she was amongst new peers; folks who seemed to be much more computer and internet inclined than she. These feelings showed mostly when she was asked to perform in class and or write a paper for the college writing class she was also taking. Yes, she was attending the non-profit program of study as well as a community college part-time. This girl was either serious or crazy! The fear that she felt most days was totally beyond anything that she in and of herself could conquer; all she could do was rely on God to see her through.

Chapter 22

Thank God there was one person in the class who really knew her and she never missed an opportunity to encourage and build Becky up, it was Tara, they met in rehab. She and this young lady had started out together in their new lives, and they grew together in everything. Soon she was graduating from the computer class and adding another notch in her belt of things she started and actually completed. She now could give college her all and she did just that. She was at the top of her class at Prince George's Community College in Largo, Maryland. She was an awesome writer; so much so that her professor mentioned the honors program to her and another young lady in the class. She began to see her gift when they were all asked to try to get letters published in one of the major newspapers. Well, wouldn't you know, she and that same young lady were published in a major paper, with Becky's letter listed first! God, this was all happening so fast she couldn't believe it. How could it be? Surely something was going to happen or go wrong. It had to! Rebecca was growing up, whether she liked it or not. She was still in awe about all that had happened in her favor to that point.

She just couldn't take it if it got any better; this is really sad: she is actually afraid to experience goodness and fruitfulness for the fear that it will go away. What a restricted life to live! It is the only life she knows and is comfortable with. She recalled the time when everyone called her about her letters that were published in the local papers. I think at that point others began to see the evidence of what they already knew. This was a talented and gifted writer. Her work just seem to flow, and it was quite simple and to the point. She kept her audiences' attention. This was a major self esteem booster for her, especially because of all the self doubt of being in class with all youngsters.

Becky got out into the working world and began to experience what it was like to be able to go to the bank without asking someone else for something and to be able to buy large-ticket items on her own. Soon she had a car of her own too! Life could not have been better. She was elated and afraid all at the same time, but decided to nurture the determination and gratitude that was inside of her instead of the low self-worth demon and the you-are-not-good-enough monster that had once taken up residency in her. She was to make it or die trying and that became her attitude. She would go on in spite of any and every thing, and believe you me she had some pretty devastating blows and some trying moments as a young woman, as a single parent, and as the sibling of folks who didn't always respect and embrace her.

She mourned the lost of some pretty important relationships early on in recovery; relationships she thought she couldn't live without. At times she wasn't sure if she would make it through the hour, much less the day. But, she felt that the love and support of those around her, and the love of God kept her. The key in her case was that she sincerely wanted to be kept, and so she was. After all, in her mind and the minds of many people she had some great excuses to go back, but she didn't through God's grace. Some how the girl who wasn't sure God even liked her noticed that she was having relations with God and it felt oh so good. She was actually relying on him all through out the day; especially when the thought of using drugs came to mind. She would catch herself saying, "God, please help me, guide me in my recovery. God, I don't want to use."

This journey that she was on had taken twist and turns she never imagined possible. Her life was unfolding right before her, and all she was doing was what she was led to do. Soon she began to hold her head high without being prompted by self or others; she began to speak with conviction and authority when speaking in a group, not in doubt like before. Before long she was going back over to that shelter to give some encouragement to those that were less fortunate than she. She could relate to them, because she would never forget what it felt like to be in that uncertain, stressful, and embarrassing situation. The humiliation you feel when you need to ask someone else for every little thing that you get or want to do. She was inspired to go back there because of all that God had done for her and her family. In her mind she was the worst of the worst, and if God and the program could help her, anybody could be helped. That was her message. If she could step outside of the chains of abuse, low self-worth, no self-worth, rape, domestic violence, alcohol and drugs, molestation and incest, anybody could be free. This overwhelms her even as she speaks about it today and not just the pain of it but the beauty as well. She knows that God truly does love her today, and that he blesses her beyond measure in spite of all the mistakes she has made (some of which she truly believes were sketched out for her and not at all by chance).

The scares of her yesterday don't determine her todays or her tomorrows; she refuses to allow that to happen. She really does exemplify the scripture; you can do all things through Christ who strengthens you. She gets emotional when she embraces the fact that she really is blessed and highly favored.

As she took the life skills training classes back to that shelter, her esteem grew and soon she realized that she had a secret admirer. She was in a state of shock and disbelief.

Chapter 23

Although he made it known he was interested a few years prior, she didn't think it was so genuine. She was elated, and afraid; what was she going to do? Was this guy serious? What was it about her that made him so interested in her? All these questions and more went through Becky's mind on a regular basis. Well, for once in her life she listened to that inner voice before she made any decisions. She decided to enjoy the sheer pleasure of this guy's gestures toward her and to do nothing, and see just how long it would last. This seemed like a good idea for someone like Becky because she was always looking to be loved. She had always been a very affectionate child even though she'd been molested. It didn't take away her nurturing and caring attitude.

Surprisingly, this guy did not give up, yet he never pressured her. This was amazing to Becky, and another self esteem booster. She was finding out some great things about herself and life. She seemed to be on a journey of epiphany—a Greek word for revelation or manifestation. Boy was she discovering some beautiful things, especially about herself! The pain of being dark skinned didn't live in her anymore, she no longer wished she had smaller lips, and she understood that there was actually nothing wrong with being 5 feet 7 inches tall. She began discovering her own self-worth and beauty without basing it on anybody else and it felt good. She realized that God had delivered her from some pretty demonic spirits.

Given her history it was only God's grace and his mercy that she was in her right frame of mind, and that all of the injustice she had endured as a young girl was no longer imprisoning her. She was not bound in her heart, shackled in her mind, and her soul was no longer incarcerated. She was actually free to live, to experience, to love, to grow, to make mistakes, to give, and to mirror to others the true miracle of God's love in her life. This was a major transformation for a girl who felt nothing at one point except fear, anger and pain.

Hallelujah is an order on that note, praise be to God and to God be all the glory! It is important to give credit where it is due because without him Becky realizes that she would be nothing. As she allows the tears to flow from her eyes, she relives some of the most horrific moments of her life and shares a few with me. She advises of the time someone ran over her legs, as she jumped from a moving car to escape being raped. Not one bone in her body was broken. Then there were all the times she barely escaped death. But there is one time in particular that really showed her that God is with her. She stood side by side with someone trying to retrieve something that belonged to her and for some reason she felt a stirring in her spirit telling her to move, just go, and so she did. Before she could even cross the street, gunshots rang out and her friend laid dead in the alleyway. She had not taken more than 25 steps and boom; just like that she stayed alive.

This brings to mind stories such as The Ugly Duckling and Cinderella. It's not so much in the physical but in the spirit. Although she did grow up to be an extremely beautiful black woman inside and out, she went from doubt, anger, and fear to assured, pleasant, and able. She walked away from envy and jealousy and into: can you show me how to do that? Can I come too? What an enormous transformation! She finally realized the freedom that comes from letting go and letting God. She was experiencing the relief that comes with believing that God could and would if he was sought.

All of the things she learned started to manifest in her daily life; she saw the need to rely on this information on a regular basis and she also witnessed the fruit of her actions too—good and bad. Clearly she began to see that early on she didn't do better because she didn't know better. Her circumstances were very, very scary and painful; it was embarrassing for her to know that someone raped her, that they ejaculated in her face, and that they treated her like a dirty old rag. It was painful to think about all the guys that seemed to come into contact with you with the same agenda. She was their sex object. They touched, they felt, they tampered, they dug, and they poked and banged on her. As a child, how do you make proper sense out of something like that? At five, how do you let go and let God? All the church going in the world wouldn't help. This spirit formed a personality in her that would hold her captive for years and the damage would prove to almost be irreversible. But God.

Doomed to be Nothing, Destined to be Something

Leaving all those negative feelings and spirits behind proved to be more challenging than she ever feared, because the haters were out there and some of them weren't about to let her forget. Honey, they reminded her every chance they got that she wasn't this or that or that she wasn't going to ever be anything. When you go to a self help group they tell you to remember your story, well she didn't have to worry about that because folks in her life remembered it for her and reminded her any time it looked like she thought she was something or somebody. It was almost like, how dare you think something of your self and then to top it off; hold your head high? The kicker came whenever she spoke highly of herself. She learned early on from a woman in the shelter, that people can take back the hammer anytime they want to by not allowing others to hold you hostage to the past. God forgives us and throws our sins and mistakes into the sea of forgetfulness, so why can't humans? She said whatever horrible, shameful things she may have done in the past, she embraces it, she owns it, and she moves on. If you want, she said, bring it and use it as a whipping tool if you want to, and she'll just take it out of your hands. She calls it the "yes, I did do that, and it was absolutely horrible" syndrome. She said doing that takes all power away from those who think they're going to hold her captive with the past. "Oh, it felt so good the first time that I did it too". The woman who she first practiced this with just stood there like, "hey, I'm suppose to be saying those horrible things about you, not you!"

God is a healer and a deliverer and he will keep you in perfect peace. The song Never Would Have Made It by Marvin Sapp comes to mind whenever Becky now thinks about this portion of her journey. Soon, Rebecca started to become affected by Mr. Clark's interest in her; he is the secret admirer from the shelter. She began rehearsing in her mind what she was going to say to him. At this point, some years had gone by and he was still asking about her and this really flattered her. It told her something about him too—that he was obviously not giving up, and that his interest in her was sincere. Well, she got this bright idea and asked Zina to go with her to see him at work one day, flowers in hand. When she got there and took the long walk up the sidewalk, she could see him watching her and almost passed out. She was trying to get there as fast as she could! Once inside she handed him a bush of flowers. He looked so shocked that they were for him, but seemed extremely happy to see her. That night they talked on the phone almost all night, and she went into work the next day with what felt like a hangover. She had never been so elated in her life or stimulated like that by conversation. Oh my God is what she thought! This was actually one of the counselors that she had met early on in her journey that seem to be so fond of her. He seemed to have so much admiration and confidence in her. Even though it was new to her, she went with it and enjoyed the experience.

Doomed to be Nothing, Destined to be Something

Chapter 24

What she didn't know was that he had been hurt pretty badly in his life too and that her purpose in his life wasn't what either of them thought. For Becky it was totally beyond her to think that God could have another purpose for her in Clark's life other than the obvious. The love that God allowed this girl to hold in her heart for others was enormous and totally beyond any human power. All of the pain she had endured up to this point was preparation to understand, nurture and love. In return she got to experience being loved and allowing someone to come in.

This relationship was like being in a hallway that didn't always have lights. She turned many corners without knowing what she was going to meet. This was the first sign that Becky suffered from the nervousness and unmanageability of her youth even in her adult life. When she was overwhelmed, hurting or afraid, she would always panic and seek to fix it at all costs. Many times this annoyed the hell out of those closest to her. She didn't seem to be able to let go and let God. It was like a chain reaction and she didn't seem to be able to see until afterwards that the fear of things going on took her outside of her faith in God and back to those days of domestic violence with her mom; back to the rapes and molestation, and back to days where she was physically abused herself and didn't know how to get out. This was a fear and anxiety that Clark's issues seem to magnify.

Most days she exercised her faith and the glory of God in her life. But somehow those things didn't seem to click so fast in matters of the heart and love. She was so connected to this man that all of her wisdom and knowledge was at his mercy and if they didn't have a good day, her faith didn't seem to be as great. This pained her heart because she knew that God was real and that she was able to do exceedingly and abundantly above all that she could think or imagine, because of the evidence of her life. What could her blockage be? Where did she go wrong? What happened to her and her father's (God) relationship? Why wasn't she relying on him like before? It almost seemed like God wasn't working with her anymore. Where was all of the difficulty, pain and drama really coming from? Why wasn't that miraculous power interceding on her behalf anymore?

She had a lot of time to think about this during the course of her long journey with Clark. They shared a very, very intimate and spiritual bond and they could talk about anything; sometimes to a fault. Becky really felt good about their relationship, but soon learned that her love wasn't enough to heal his hurting heart or enough to restore his confidence in a woman again. Apparently her issues around safety, given all that she had been through, proved to be a challenge for Clark as well. His anger and fear pushed her away and her not feeling safe caused her to hold on tighter. Although they hurt each other, there was never a time when it felt malicious or intentional. This is what made the bond so close and the feelings so unique for Clark and Becky. He was hurt by the woman he trusted the most, and therefore whenever he allowed himself to experience the real love Becky had for him; he was very, very elated too. She was able to embrace him in a new way, because for the most part he was only the second man who came along who didn't make a big deal over sexing her up. Jerry was the first, and it felt really good to be treated like a lady and like a prize. Clark looked at her with such admiration and interest; he listened to her as she shared her experiences and often times held her as she cried. When he found out about the viciousness of the rapes and molestation she went through, he took it upon himself to take responsibility for what other men had done to her. I am sure you are wondering how he could do this. Well, he did and it was just what the doctor had ordered for this woman's fragile heart.

Early in their relationship, he asked if he could play a movie for her one afternoon and she said yes. As the movie began to play, he left the room. Much to her surprise it was a movie called Sister I'm Sorry. In the story line famous men, one after another, appeared on the screen apologizing for raping, abandoning, beating, molesting, prostituting, deceiving, exploiting, disrespecting and introducing women to drugs. They were sincerely and humbly pleading to women for forgiveness of such cowardly acts toward them. For the first time in her life, someone had actually taken responsibility for what had been done to her. She cried a river that day and Clark came back into the living room and began wiping the tears from her eyes. He didn't say anything, just held her as she wept.

Rebecca and Clark planned to marry and announced it to the world. They proceeded to make arrangements for the wedding and she enjoyed every moment of it. She had her Matron of Honor go with her to pick out her dress; it was the most special moment of her life as her cousin Sheila stood in that bridal shop and the reality of her dream unfolded. She made her final selection and couldn't wait to share it with Clark. He was elated any time they talked about their wedding. He was very interested in all of her babbling about the details and everything.

    Just when things couldn't be better, they moved in together—something Becky vowed not to do. Things were awesome at first, but then something seemed to go wrong. They thought it was this and they thought it was that, but she says she now knows that it was God's unfailing love for her that was interceding. Though she and Clark loved each other deeply, neither of them included God in their day to day interactions, as a couple. They never made the types of commitments about fornication that they should have. These were just a few of the reasons why she felt their relationship wasn't as fruitful as it could have been. Despite all hell breaking loose, they hung in there and gave it everything they had. They gave and gave until there was nothing left to give, and finally in 2005 they called it quits. But it was not before Rebecca made a complete mess out of things in October 2003 and continued into 2004.

Chapter 25

Rebecca found her self hurting, and alienated from Clark and in the emotional embrace of another man. This was crucial because Clark seemed to sincerely want to work things out with her. She asked for some time to think and he honored her request, although he was devastated. She loved him enough though to allow him to come into therapy with her, after he gave her time and space for 30 days. Soon they reconciled and began trying to put the pieces back together but it was never the same. Rebecca did the exact same thing again; she overlooked the greatest man ever one more time; her father in heaven.

She kept searching for love, acceptance, companionship, relations, and that spiritual and emotional embrace that came from physical relationships. Soon she realized she wasn't going to be able to get it. She just wanted to feel safe, in every sense of the word. Just when it seemed things couldn't get any worse, Jerry had a heart attack and stroke while on a trip to California. She would never forget it; she remembers it like it was yesterday. It was one of the worst feelings she has ever felt, knowing that she was really his only family. What in the world was she going to do? The first thing was to get to California to see how bad it was. Not sure if he was going to make it, Rebecca was devastated and only held on by the grace of God.

She just continued trusting God in all of it, even though she couldn't seem to do that in her relations with Clark. At this point, she knew intuitively that she was incapable of loving two men at once. Each time she fell in love with a man, she seemed to fall out of love with God. She would still love, but not be in love anymore. This was terribly humiliating and she didn't know what to do about it. She was ashamed and very embarrassed by it because she knew she should know better. After all that God had brought her through, how could she neglect and abandon him that way? Her personal savior! He had to love and honor her because of all He had delivered her from. He sustained her in some of the most horrific circumstances. He protected her little mind when she was a small girl, he safe guarded her nurturing loving spirit, and he gave her an attitude of determination throughout it all. She was going to beat this thing one way or another. If anyone was worthy of such a commitment from her, surely it was God. It was going to be harder than she ever imagined because her relationship with God was not tangible.

With a made up mind, Rebecca began to embrace the idea of being alone and without Clark. She really was scared to death while on her trip to California. Things didn't look to good for Jerry; he didn't recognize anyone, looked terrible, and was just like a newborn baby. The hospital that they moved him to once he was out of imminent danger was just terrible. Instead of being able to concentrate on the matter at hand, Becky was extremely worried about things back at home with Clark and the kids. She and Clark had been bickering and she didn't feel good about leaving that way. She left California feeling overwhelmed by all the things the hospital told her she needed to get done for Jerry. She was an emotional wreck, and didn't see any relief in site.

She returned to Maryland only to find more fuel to add to the fire. She and Clark never spoke again after that day. She really didn't have the energy to give to such a trying and delicate situation. She just gave up completely, and convinced herself that she would be better off without the drama that seemed to follow her and Clark. Love just wasn't enough anymore. Now afraid and alone for real, she wondered how she would tell the children about what had happened to Jerry. They were already wondering why he never called them or answered his cell phone. Becky lied repeatedly during the days leading up to her leaving for California. She told one lie after another; she just couldn't bring herself to tell them such horrendous news, about the man they simply adored. She sought spiritual and Godly counsel before speaking with the children. When she finally spoke to them, it didn't go as badly as she had anticipated. Of course they had lots of questions, were saddened, and wanted to know when he was going to come home. She responded to them by being as honest as humanly possible; explaining to them that prayer was the best thing they could give to Jerry.

Mind you, while this situation was continuing, she still had to return to work the next day. How in the world was she going to manage all by herself? Who would she be able to count on? Who could she trust, and how much should she trust them? When was her heart going to stop hurting, when? If she was ever going to get through this she would have to reestablish her self with the most high. It was difficult because she had an emotional blockage and spiritual pit that she had fallen into and she wasn't sure how to get out of it. It was almost like she was reaching up and out, but couldn't grab a hold of anything. For her own sake she had to keep reaching though.

Eventually she found herself resting, being at peace, casting her cares on God again, expecting a miracle, and also she saw the stepping stones made of stumbling blocks manifest in her, the family, and in her life. Once afraid and baffled, she was now free again and unafraid of what the future held. She believed it was already alright and that she could do it; she was going to make it after all. Seemingly, being alone always afforded her the best opportunity possible to get to know the Lord. She would always put other folks and other things in front of him. That's why she kept losing them. If she was going to be happy, she would definitely have to learn to allow God to be God in her life and to let Him reign in all her relations. Talk about challenging! That is an understatement to say the least. Men have always had an influence over her that only God should have. This woman was wide open at this point, ripe for God. When everything else failed, she went looking for God and He heard her cry.

Thankful and emotional; but she continued discussing this area of her life. She has an enthusiasm today that she never knew before. It was a long time coming, but change was happening. Rebecca began to talk about the things that happened along her walk that made her the woman she is today. Well, remember all the bad experiences she had with men, especially as a child? She felt so used and abused, so ugly and nasty. Well to God be the glory, this same women began to walk with confidence.

Becky recalls a time when she and a very, very close relative went for jobs. There were about six people in the room all trying to get the same job. They only had three positions available. Well, she sat and listened to everybody talk about how expensive their résumé paper was, about their wealth of experience, and various college degrees. She wanted to disappear and just leave, going up against all these knowledgeable and capable people. Surely she wasn't going to get the job; she had no experience, no degrees, and the paper she'd typed her résumé on was just plain cheap. After they took the test, the recruiter advised when he came back he would call off some names and those people were to come with him. Sure enough, when he came back he called off three names and those people left the room. Well there she sat, feeling like a failure because her name wasn't called; but then she looked around and realized that she was left in the room with the college graduates. She thought to her self, how in the world did they not get the job and what in the world was she still doing in the room with them? Much to her surprise, the recruiter returned and congratulated them on their new jobs. She was in total shock! He had to be mistaken. Oh my God, she said, She had actually out scored all the other applicants, and one of the college graduates.

Doomed to be Nothing, Destined to be Something

Chapter 26

Then there was the time she worked for this really great organization but her supervisor was under investigation and would have to test on all software that his team used. He was frightened out of his mind so much so that he knew he would have to get help. He called Becky in on her day off for double time and a half to sit with him while he tested. She coached him and he passed with flying colors. Then there was the time that her manager was asked for his best rep to assist with a major project for the president's office. Well, he chose Becky. He also sent her to train other representatives to assist in the quality assurance department and eventually recommended her for a promotion after only a few months of being with the company. She received enormous bonuses and was recognized repeatedly amongst her peers and internal and external customers again and again.

However, the thing that stands out the most to her about this time is the fact that she would never get on the elevator because of the discomfort she felt when standing with men. She could not take the bad, insecure, nervous, and scary feelings she experienced on what seemed to be the longest elevator rides of her life. She began taking the stairs. She was still struggling with the things those God-awful men did to her when she was a little girl. Her breathing would change while in closed quarters, and it always felt like the dizziness was going to cause her to faint. At some point during these episodes, she got a position as a chairperson at a 12 step group—a position she would never have taken on her own. It took a senior member of the group to nominate her. To her surprise, she accepted, mainly because she knew that Clark would be by her side. Rebecca had no idea how that commitment would change her life.

She showed up every week and was the only women there. It was Rebecca and a room full of men each and every Sunday. Of course she had the same feelings there as she did on the elevator; oh, but God! She sat most times with her head hung down, twittling her fingers until the end of the meeting. But, soon she gained the confidence to speak and to tell those guys what was wrong with her. She told them exactly how she felt in that room with them each and every Sunday. And then one day she said, "I forgive all of you for the things you may have done to hurt other woman in your life". I am forgiving you for rape, for molestation, for domestic violence, and for feeding woman drugs in order to exploit and take advantage of them." She continued, "I forgive you all because I need to be forgiven."

It seemed like a weight was lifted from her that day and she acquired a renewed confidence. Here is the kicker though; soon she got on that elevator at work and said good morning to the men while holding her head high. She never took the steps again unless she just wanted the exercise. She remained at that meetings with those men for about 3 years and after being there for about 1 year or so, other women began to come. God gave her that time to be healed by the great respect and admiration that this wonderful group of guys had for her. They encouraged her, they supported her, they tolerated her, they guided her, and they had faith in her recovery. After being a part of that group, she would never be the same, and certainly not held hostage by the past anymore. She would be eternally grateful to those men for they have no idea what they were able to accomplish. They had worked a miracle with help from God in this woman.

Now she was ready to face life on her terms. She understood that she could not blame all men for what some had done and also that there were some great men in this world. God had afforded her the opportunity to cross paths with a few of them, Clark included. What more could she ask for? She never thought she could be free of the residue of the injustice she faced growing up, and always wondered: How could she ever think anything of herself? Why would men ever respect her with all of the baggage she had to carry up until that point? Why was she worthy of such a blessing like freedom from her past? God really did give her favor and it was just that simple. She was chosen; she was blessed and could have never thought these things up. These are just a few of the things that kept her grounded and willing to stand up when she should fall. This is the type of evidence that wouldn't allow her to go back. It motivates and builds her up, no longer allowing the past to tear her down. She now honors God with all that she knows how; yet, she seeks to get a better understanding of his word and purpose for her in this life. She never thought she would be anything, yet felt like something good. With all of the destruction, abuse, and rape she encountered, her path had always looked dark. She would never have made it if she didn't have concrete evidence to hold on to. What would all that she had been through mean in her new life? How was it all relevant to what it was God intended for her to do? She was always seeking to know her purpose and to understand why God saved her from so many things. Why did he choose her and not some of the women who died on the streets?

Chapter 27

Soon she began to feel like her purpose was being revealed. She crossed paths with a lost, hurting, and confused young lady. This proved to be the test of all time for Becky. Now she would have to put all the compassion she ever felt from God and man to the test. She would have to be a light leading out of darkness for this woman, her name was Samantha. She revealed to Becky that she was involved in prostitution and that she felt embarrassed to go around any of her family. She feared they would all reject and judge her, and they would make her an outcast. God is good, because Becky knew that feeling and that same fear; she always felt like she would be an outcast if she ever told anybody what she had really endured in her short life time because she thought it would make her look bad. She really felt like folks in her family looked down on her for getting on drugs, being as smart as she was. They had no idea how much her soul ached, or just how empty she really felt. She could feel Sam's pain and they seemed to have a bond beyond any that Sam had ever known.

Becky and Samantha became so close until Becky found herself going out all hours of the night to rescue Sam from beatings from her pimp. She received calls in the wee hours of the morning as Samantha ran through alleys, escaping being raped or killed. She found out that this girl's long and beautiful hair was cut off by a pimp as punishment for running away. One night Sam called Becky and said "I can't even do wrong right; I just don't seem to fit in and that's why I keep changing pimps". Becky told her on that day that the reason she didn't fit in was because she wasn't like the other girls, and that God had another purpose for her. She explained to Sam how God would never allow her to fit into that arena; because of the plans he had for her.

Becky would visit the track or the street corner where Sam was working just to let her know that she loved her and that she was praying for her speedy return to her family and the Lord. Seeing this young woman through required a lot more time than Becky could have ever imagined. This girl's tolerance for pain was great. She had to go through a lot more than Becky hoped before she would get out.

After a few years of leaving and going back, Becky told her that she would no longer come to get her, but that she would always be welcome at her house. She would have to make her own way there though. She put it back on her, just to see how badly she wanted out. Knowing how much Becky loved her, Samantha tried to get her to come out one more time and Becky said NO. After a day or two had gone by, an unexpected knock came at the door and it was Sam. With her emotions running on high, Rebecca grabbed that girl and held her tight. She could feel the love of God in the room and a stirring in her spirit. They just cried as they embraced one another. God was really proving himself to Becky in all of this; she felt as if she was really, really related to Him, like his child for real, and she knew why he spared her. It was to do the work of building his kingdom and to be a light for those who are lost, in trying to find their way home.

It was all happening so fast and she had gone from this scared, empty vessel to a courageous, bona fide, and faithful servant. She was willing to do whatever she had to in order for this young girl to experience the kind of healing and freedom she had. Rebecca took on the challenge of a frightened, dishonest, intoxicated, unstable young woman. She embraced her with all the love in her heart. Too bad it wasn't enough to completely turn her around. She would have to solicit God's help with that. There were points in time where Sam had no idea of the affects of her lifestyle and behavior on Becky. Zina eventually enlightened her and let her know just how bad Becky was really doing. It had gotten to the point where she had to take pills to go to sleep, pills to get up, and pills to function. She kept reliving the horrors of some of the late night phone calls with Sam screaming and crying about barely escaping rape and robbery.

Sam was always trying to hide from the police, and not for fear of going to jail, but of being raped and robbed. She was tired of being raped by them! Yes, raped—sex in exchange for not going to jail. This troubled Becky terribly and she always feared for Sam's life. She realized that she had to let go and let God though, because she and her family were beginning to suffer over things that were really not theirs. She created a prayer box and wrote out her prayers for Samantha and placed them in the box. It wasn't until then that she got some relief. She knew in her heart of hearts that Sam was hurting, lost, confused, and felt trapped.

Sam shared with Becky that she may die if she tried to leave her pimp. However, Becky declared that she almost died staying with him too. But to God be the glory, one night a fight broke out between the pimp and another man. The man returned with a gun and opened fire on the pimp and all of his ladies; supposedly Sam included, hitting several of them. Sure enough, homicide police began calling around asking someone to come to identify Sam's body. After trying to reach other relatives, they called Becky and asked if she would come down. Becky calmly put down the phone, began to breathe in and out slowly, meditating on her prayers for that girl and on the mighty name of Jesus. She picked up the receiver and called Clark, yes Clark, and informed him of what had just happened. She told him that she would not be going down to ID the body and asked if he would go. He said yes, and so she waited for him to advise.

All she could do was cry when she got the news that it really wasn't Sam and that she was ok. One of the women killed had Sam's identification in her purse and therefore the police assumed she was the victim. Becky began petitioning God on behalf of Sam. She asked for divine intervention and deliverance, and claimed it. Wouldn't you know, before long that girl declared that she didn't fit in out there and that she was tired of that life style. She simply asked if Becky would stand by her, guide and support her, and love and accept her. Rebecca accepted her with open arms.

The pain of being born again in her own life gave Rebecca the strength and determination to stand in the face of adversity with Sam. Sam had a lot of very, very unhealthy mentalities and her heart was hardened by the mean streets of Washington, DC.

    Rebecca decided to unveil some of her own skeletons with Sam, just to convey to her that she was not alone, to show her that God was a keeper if you wanted to be kept. She wanted Sam to know that she could turn her circumstances around if she followed the law of God. In order to turn it around, she would have to "seek ye first, the kingdom of God and all of his righteousness and everything else would be added unto her". Using the bible was iffy with her because she was so far away from God, so much so that he almost didn't exist to Sam anymore. Becky would be the only church, bible, or self help group that this poor child would see. She knew that it was extremely important to let Sam know that she would never judge her and that no matter what mistakes she made, she would never turn her back on her. Becky told Sam that she would never walk away from her because God never left her; despite some of the God-awful mistakes she had made.

Doomed to be Nothing, Destined to be Something

Chapter 28

At some point during Sam's journey with Becky, they talked about self esteem and Becky told Sam that she had a brother that never really liked her because of the color of her skin, and that he would always say she wasn't his sister. He even went as far as to say that the hospital sent Venis home with the wrong baby. This hurt Becky's self esteem more than any of the pain that she had ever endured early on. They cried together while talking about this and Sam said she didn't like looking like her dad, that she didn't like her features, and that one good thing came out of using those drugs: she lost weight. This admission saddened Becky terribly and she appealed to Sam to embrace herself the way that God had made her. She reiterated to Sam that she was beautiful, intelligent, and much more capable than she could ever imagine. Sam's reply was, "but I'm not strong like you Becky. You can't expect me to make it because you did. I am just screwed up, and I can't seem to do anything right." Becky interrupted her and said, "No, you can't do wrong right, Sweetie."

Right in the middle of this conversation, which seemed to be coming to an end, there was a pulling at Becky's heart and she decided to share about a very hurtful and frightening event in her life as a young girl. Even at this stage in her life, she still felt wounded by that particular tragedy. It was one of the things that let her know that there had to be a God somewhere. All she could remember was the moment when three black men caught her walking on a dark street in southeast DC and kidnapped her. She knew the moment they pulled her into that car that her life was over. She was most cooperative and did everything they told her to do; and I do mean everything! What an encounter for a seventeen year old girl? They took her to a dark, remote area off of Suitland Parkway to a wooded area. Once out of the car, she was thrown down onto a filthy, nasty, smelly mattress. She was very fragile and emotional at the time, and to make matters worse; she was on her menstrual cycle. She laid there in total disbelief at gun point as the first guy jumped on her pounding and pounding, ooing and aahing, until his relief came. Then the next guy took his turn and came up, out and off of her all bloody. When it came time for the last guy to get his turn with her, he had a sudden change of heart. Right before the second guy could get up, Rebecca noticed that the third guy turned the gun on the second guy. Instead of getting his turn, he yelled, "Let her up, man! Let her go"!

Once in the car he began wiping all of the blood and bodily fluids off of Becky. He kept asking her if she was okay and where she wanted to go and she said to Goodhope Road and Minnesota Avenue. Still holding the gun, he ordered the driver to take her where she wanted to go. He apologized for what they did to her, and began taunting his partners in crime. He said we, meaning the guys, should be ashamed of ourselves because we got women waiting on us, we should have just gone to 51 (a local liquor store) and came back. The store was not far from where they took her to rape her. She was extremely grateful for the chance to walk away from that. She was hurting something terrible down there and was bleeding pervusively. She just wanted to get to her cousin Sheila's house and take a bath. All the way there, it felt like she was going to pass out but she didn't. She prayed all the way there; asking God to please allow her to make it there and He did. The problem was that once there, Sheila opened the door and was obviously very high off some form of narcotic. She never once asked what happened. She opened the door, closed it, and went back into a nod. This made Becky feel even more horrible. After all, she looked up to Sheila and expected that she would hold her, wipe the tears from her eyes, or something. Rebecca went straight into the bathroom, where Sheila found her the next morning, asleep. She had soaked all evidence away at this point and never bothered to tell her cousin anything. All she could think about was if only her mom hadn't put her out the night before, none of this would have happened to her.

Eventually she called her mom, who was visiting with a friend for an extended stay and asked if she could come. Her mom said yes and off she went. For the next 2 days, she lay in bed with a temperature of 104 and eventually unable to walk due to the tremendous abdominal pains she was having from all of the pounding and banging those guys had done to her the night before. Well the sicker she got, the more afraid her mom became; so she rushed her to Hadley Memorial hospital in SE DC. Once at the hospital, the doctors advised her mom that her daughter had three different sexually transmitted diseases. Thank God AIDS wasn't around back then.

Becky just told Sam that this was devastating to her, and that it made her feel like used goods, insecure, and less than worthy at times, and that god had instilled in her that she was all that he said she was! She shared that god had imparted in her spirit that none of it was her fault; she explained how relieved she was to be free of that bondage. Becky told Sam that she had to will and purpose in her heart to love, respect, and appreciate herself and that it didn't happen overnight, but it happened. She told her that it could happen for her as well.

That night at the hospital Venis was sick with regret when she realized what had happened to her daughter and that it happened on the night that she put her out on the streets. Sadly though, she couldn't bring herself to tell Becky how sorry she really was; but Becky knowing her mom that way she did, could see it in her eyes and feel it in her touch. This is a prime example of why Clark's efforts to say I'm sorry to her through the Sister I'm Sorry movie were so therapeutic. Rebecca felt a connection to Clark that she knew would always be there; however, as you remember they never married despite the high esteem they held for one another. For Becky, this was especially important because she allowed God to order her steps as far as this was concerned. She often wondered why she had to endure so much pain, why so much tragedy at such a young age? She shared with Sam that the words, Why, why, why haunted her at times because as much as she knew there was a God, her flesh couldn't resist the urge to question Him or His existence; where was he during all of those horrible things that happened to her? She silently thought to herself, either I am just that horrible of a creature, or God is just plain ole mean. She felt cut off at a very early age; she never really felt the song she so often sang: "Jesus loves me. This I know, for the bible tells me so." Becky says she never felt so left out in her whole life as she did when singing that song. How could God love her and watch as she was being raped, molested, and ejaculated on? And in her face at that!!!

Samantha asked Becky, how in the world do you tell a 5, 6, or 7 year old that Jesus loves them and they understand it under those conditions? Becky was taken back by her question, and could only offer this: all things worked together for the good of them that loved the lord and are called according to his purpose. She hoped with all her heart that Sam received this message and could truly understand it. Becky wished that Sam could see the glory of the Lord as it shined in Becky's life as they spoke.

This woman was a true miracle; she really, really was and Sam felt blessed to know her and to have witnessed her story unfold. She gave her a kind of hope that she had never known before. To this day, she is a walking testimony in and of herself about the goodness of the Lord. Becky is light in darkness, and she is strength in times of sorrow, trouble, and heartache. She should be an encouragement to us all. She doesn't feel sorry for herself or solicit pity from others. She has embraced her life the way that it is and accepts her past the way that it was.

She allows God to use her in the lives of the broken and the lost. She considers it an honor and a privilege to help somebody else. She has turned what Satan had meant bad into something sweet and wonderful, by allowing God to get the glory out of what seemed to be her impending doom. She does not proclaim that the road was easy or is easy, because it is not. Her message is simple, and it is that God is all that she needs in order to endure all things. Notice she says to endure all things and not avoid them, because if God is truly going to get the glory, she knows that she is going to have to go through something. Without her test, she has no testimony.

Chapter 29

Now was the time for Becky to let go and let God's will be done in Samantha. She has done what God would have her to do. She would continue to be a light for Sam, but also allow God to work in her and be manifested in any way He sees fit. Samantha would have to suffer a little while longer though and Rebecca wiped many more tears from her eyes, but God is an on time God!

Becky also began to serve in this same role for others. She recalls a time when she felt so much compassion for her brother Dave, who did everything imaginable to destroy her self worth and self esteem as a child. For some reason, she was able to care for him with everything that she had. Each time he went to jail her heart ached, and every time she witnessed him in that nod from the heroin, she hurt. Each time those men on the street beat the crap out of him and he was rescued only by jail, she hurt. Rebecca believed that love was what God would have her do concerning her brother, although many times he was used as her attacker by the enemy.

Looking back over her life now, she understands that the enemy must have seen her worth long before she had the chance to discover it and that would explain the all out attack on her life from the very beginning. If only she had known while enduring and going through it, she would have praised and thanked God in advance for every trial and every tribulation that resulted in her becoming the phenomenal women that she is. There is one specific incident that Rebecca recalls involving Dave, the oldest of Venis's kids. As she prepared for bed one night, the tears rolled down her face. She silently thanked God for all that He had done for her, while remembering some moments of divine intervention for her brother. She thought about the time when she and Pastor X were on their way to do some things that they should not have been doing, but the Lord stepped in. Unfortunately, it was in a way that she wouldn't wish on anybody.

While in route to do wrong, she noticed her brother creeping on the train tracks with a guy who was no good! This was strange because her brother had kicked his heroine addiction and was headed in the right direction, and to see him with this creep was bad news. For this reason, she stopped dead in her tracks to go to her brother's aid instead of getting high and getting laid. Pastor X and getting high would just have to wait. She followed her brother back to the development where they lived. When she got to the house, he was no where to be found. However, Becky had a pretty good idea of where she could find him. What she found devastated her! She knocked on the door of the home of the guy he was creeping with and was told through a closed door, that her brother was not there. Her heart sunk at that point because she feared she may not catch him before he did something stupid. Her brother's decision to stop shooting up was one of the best decisions he had made in a long time and if she could, she wanted to encourage and support him; even though she was battling a like-minded demon.

Doomed to be Nothing, Destined to be Something

At that point in her life, she was getting high even though she really wanted to stop, and although it made her feel worse than she did prior to using the stuff. The feelings that she was trying to escape were more bearable than the ones she was left with after getting loaded. She used because she felt bad and had to keep using because it made her feel worse. It was almost like being afraid to live, but more afraid of dying. Darned if you do and damned if you don't. Using to live, living to use, and being trapped in a vicious cycle.

Doomed to be Nothing, Destined to be Something

Chapter 30

She recalls walking away from that guy's door, wondering where her brother could be. Something told her to peak through the crack in the shade and so she did. She saw her brother's shoes, socks, and clothing scattered around the room and she knew right then and there that he was in trouble! She screamed and banged on that door over and over until somebody answered. She called for her mom to come because she found her brother overdosed in a tub, naked while the folks in the house were all so high they couldn't even communicate. They were all in a simultaneous nod. Venis had nursing experience and knew exactly what to do to bring her child back. She iced him down, dressed him, and they took him home because he refused medical help.

Life for most people never reaches lows like this, but this was a way of life for Rebecca—hopelessness every day and every night. What was going to become of her and her family who were all falling victim to drugs and alcohol? This question plagued her going and coming, yet she had no answers. The other sad part of all of this is that Zina was watching the simultaneous demise of all of her loved ones.

A few hours after Rebecca and Venis rescued him, David finished up the rest of the heroine that almost killed him. For Becky, it was almost as if her brother's lack of success with his addiction somehow directly affected her outlook on her own battle. Full of uncertainty and boat loads of fear, Rebecca continued the destructive pattern she wanted so desperately to be rid of but couldn't. The only hope she had left was in the silent prayer in her heart, for God to hear and feel her pain. She so badly wished to pray out loud but could not. Her words were silenced by her pain. Surprisingly, somehow Becky held on to the thought that one day God would rescue her from herself, from her past, and from the vultures that sought to devour her out there in those streets. She wondered about the out come of all of the nasty and deceitful men that preyed on her; her whole life. When you have suffered your whole life, and poverty and despair is all around you, how do you break free of the chains? These were Becky's thoughts and feelings all of the time. How, how, how? When would she be able to live a normal life, when would the time come that she could feel good in her skin and be free of the fumes of the molestation all over her? When would the nightmares of the rapes and beatings be replaced with more pleasant memories? How would she make it over? She often wondered if Dr. Martin Luther King's words—"We will get to the promise land"—had anything to do with all of the injustice she faced as a child? She wondered if those words had escaped her? The fear of being trapped in a life that bore little or no resemblance of joy, freedom, light, or peace overwhelmed this young girl on a regular basis. Without a light of her own to follow, she fell deeper and deeper into states of panic and depression, to desperation and degradation, guilt, and shame, sorrow, and pain. Those are the places where she resided for most of her life. She agonized over a new place to live, but did not have a clue how to get there. Coming from a family that appeared very successful made it easier to hope. It also made it easier to see how far from the standard she fell. She continued to rely on her wit and limited knowledge of God to keep her safe out in the world and inside, otherwise she would come to ruin for sure. At times she was so overwhelmed that she felt her mind pop and feared she would become someone that she didn't even recognize. She often thought that she was going to lose her mind, but God kept her although folks all around her seemed to be falling by the wayside. She wanted so badly to see past her circumstances, to know intuitively that it was going to be alright, despite what it looked like, and to feel like she was in God's unchanging hand. But she did not for a long time on the road to restoration and recovery.

Fortunately, for Becky the day came when she did realize that most of what had gone on in her life was not her fault. There wasn't a lot she could have done to change it and she should continue to use it to empower others and to share the goodness of God. She vowed to allow her life to be an example of; to whom much is given, much is required. God has given her more than she could have ever imagined and in some cases hoped for. She understands that she was chosen and that the particulars of her journey are really not important, what is important is that she made it and she was wiser, better and stronger for it. What a joy it was to be on the other side of all of that confusion and drama! If she could have, she would have poured just a small portion of the satisfaction, fulfillment, and joy on everyone with whom she came into contact so that nobody ever had to endure that type of darkness alone.

Doomed to be Nothing, Destined to be Something

Chapter 31

Rebecca is now in pursuit of a similar revelation about her present situations. She has enjoyed the revelation of the past enormously and is anticipating an even greater experience relating to right here and now, as well as her future. Juanita Bynum has a song that is often on her heart. I Don't Mind Waiting.

Recently, her life began to spiral out of control once again; she began to lose things that were dear to her, relationships that she had since childhood came to ruin despite her desire to hold on and keep them. She was informed that not only was she losing her best friends, but that her fiancé was behind it and premeditated the entire thing; he began secretly speaking with one of them over the phone for an extended period of time, and based on what they shared; turned her against Rebecca. She loved and adored this man with everything that she had, and was devastated at this news. God kept her in the midst of it all. Obviously, at times, the only ministry she had was in the form of song. She thanked God for the artists who put their real life experiences with God into the words of songs. Before she was saved, she relied on Helen Baylor's songs to keep her when she wanted to give up. She loved her songs about having a praying grandmother, and God casting our sins into the sea of forgetfulness. All of these songs were a part of her healing and her going on after one of the most horrific events in her adult life.

Rebecca grieved tremendously as she walked the author through the motivation for this book. She often walked away from its development because reliving the pain was so great and she had to do so without her two very best friends by her side. She will always love those two women but she understands that nobody came out a winner in the situation and that they too are hurt. She wants the both of them to know that if by chance they ever chose to read this book; that they will take comfort in knowing that they are both still loved and appreciated by her. It is her prayer that they find freedom and deliverance from any pain that she may have caused them. She is grateful to have had them in her life for as long as she did and she appreciates the encouragement they always gave her and their support in writing this book.

Rebecca is amazed at what God can accomplish when she avails herself to Him and she has seen the proof and rewards of her obedience in times of reluctance. She is continuing on her journey to self actualization and moving towards the light. Her hope is that men and women everywhere will find something in her story compelling enough to make them want to change, no matter if they are the victim or the culprit. Her message is that, God loves you. He is just and willing to forgive you as he has pardoned her. There is a light at the end of the tunnel although you may not see it.

She is not sure where God will have her go from this point, but she will continue to wait on God for direction and proceed with caution, humility and love .

Rebecca endured the creation of the final pages of this book on a dreary fall day, as she sat alone with a feeling of impending doom about what happened with her best friends and fiancé; agonizing about the fact that a childhood friend could leave her so easily. She realized that this book was like a pregnancy and she could not breathe easily until she had pushed it out. In telling her story she felt like she was saving her life and even though it hurt, it was a must that she get through it. Almost like she was in the labor and delivery room for the purpose of this book and she is either going to push or miscarry. She had to push pass the hurt, anger, betrayal, loneliness, rejection, depression, uncertainty and a host of other painful feelings and thoughts towards the mark of a higher calling. Rebecca declares that she is ready to proceed to the next level and knows with certainty that she must face the horrors of her actions and the destructive actions of others with courage. She must continue to labor, baring the pain of hurt, deception, backstabbing, broken heartedness, distrust, and unworthiness. She is about to take the final voyage of her book into the cobwebs of the regret and betrayal that resides in her soul, allowing others to see into her current painful reality of needing and giving forgiveness. She is standing at the door and has been for a while now, but has failed until this point to appeal to Tara and Sinai; her best friends. Rebecca had been too free with some very personal and intimate information regarding her friends with her fiancé, or with one friend about the other; although she never meant any of it maliciously. She often thought to her self, oh God; why do I have to do this, they hurt me too? Sinai began to share with Becky's fiancé about things she should never have touched, even if Becky had failed her. This was difficult, especially sense none of her offenders have ever apologized to her either, except her fiancé.

    She took a look at her past regarding all of the injustice she endured and fought to overcome in order to get an idea of how to survive all of this. First, she had to stop thinking of herself and think of Christ on the cross. She had to remember all that God had done for her and she had to embrace all of the guardian angels He had placed in her life. She had to humbly submit to He who is ruler over her life. This was very difficult for her, it was painful and in some ways it was humiliating, but it was necessary for her development and growth. She realized that she could not pick and chose where she would follow and that she had to shut up or put up.

Chapter 32

Rebecca needed to ask her childhood friend Sinai of 30 years as well as Tara for forgiveness and let Tara know that she loved and missed her, so very much; while hoping that she would offer her the same. She had to face her fiancé with the love of God and forgive him as well. Not only did she need to forgive him but she needed to cast it into the sea of forgetfulness. She must remember that the Lord is her shepherd in all things and either she was going to worship Him in spirit and in truth or she was not. This was a very, very challenging task and many times she did not understand and wanted so badly to have others understand her, but it didn't work out that way.

Rebecca was transformed as she went through each phase of this book and on her walk with God. As you can imagine, having a baby is very, very painful and this was no different. The only difference was that there was no epidural for the contractions of her fragmented self esteem, her broken heart, and distorted views of herself. She had to endure the pain in the raw. The father of this baby was no where to be found; it was the past hurts, betrayal and abuses that had impregnated her. I am sure that the loss of those relationships was the enemies plan to take her out, but God used it for her good. She was beginning to understand what it was all about: others, Christ and not her. She was able to do exceedingly and abundantly above all that she could think or imagine, at the most difficult time of her life! She returned to school, landed a great job, wrote this book, founded the Building Bridges Foundation and became very powerful in ministry.

What sacrifices was she willing to make? What pain was she willing to endure for His name sake? Would she be able to proceed with enthusiasm? Did she really believe that all things worked together for the good of those who love the Lord, and were called according to his purpose as the bible says? Did she mean it when she said that she wanted to be a light out of darkness for others?

Were there any limitations on the things she would do for the betterment of others and the uplifting of the Kingdom? Rebecca's willingness to go above and beyond will be the deciding factor in her present and future successes. Her lasting words are, "May God forgive me for anything that I have done to hurt or injure others and may I forgive and accept those who have hurt me. Rebecca declares that it is her hope that before it is all over that she is able to praise God during the storms and recognize his goodness in good and bad times, in sickness and in health, in plenty and in want. Rebecca says "I am working to be faithful over a little, so that God can make me ruler over much". Finally, she got the courage to face Tara, and as she knocked at Tara's door all she could do is pray; she was shaking and trembling so badly. In her mind it would take the favor of God to control this situation. Her heart was racing and she feels faint as Tara approaches the door; lord, have your way is what she chanted. She took a deep breath as the door opened; and submitted herself into God's hands.

Reflections

Reflections on *Doomed to be Nothing, Destined to be Something*:

It is the wish of the author that you walk away from this book renewed and empowered. Please fill out the attached pages and use them in your daily life.

- How has this book made a difference in your life?
- What stood out the most about the main character?
- How can you apply some of her characteristics into your daily dealings? Why?
- List the miracles that took place in Rebecca's life? List miracles that you now recognize have taken place in your life.
- Were you able to get a better perspective on your life? How?
- Has this story moved you to make any changes to your thoughts, behaviors, and attitudes? Please list those changes.
- Are you willing to keep a journal from this point on, so you too can see the glory of God as it unfolds in your life?
- Is there anyone to whom you need to say I'm sorry? If yes, who and will you? Once you have made your apologies, ask God to forgive you too, and then move on.

May God bless and keep you all.

Doomed to be Nothing, Destined to be Something

About The Author

Author Marsha Woodland, born in LaPlata, Maryland to the late Barbara Jean Woodland Bakr and Clarence Lee Blake is a devoted mother of four to Tarika, Tavares, Tasha, and Taliyah, a grandmother of two to B'Jean and Andrew, and a spiritual mother to many. Marsha is a God fearing woman, who declares; nothing shall separate her from the love of God. She finds fulfillment and reward in her work on the Outreach Team at her church and as a Trauma Informed Care Advocate. In doing so, she is able to witness the transformations that help, healing, and hope brings. Marsha is a true voice of the victim; in her own words, "that voice even triumphants over my own struggles and hurts." She has been able to overcome her own adversities through serving God and recognizing the needs of others. Marsha believes that it is her reasonable duty to reach back for others, and share the goodness of hope.

Currently, Marsha is a Criminal Justice Major in her third year of study at the University of Maryland University College and the proud founder of Building Bridges Foundation. Building Bridges serves the needs of female ex-offenders in the Washington D.C. metropolitan area because they too are victims. To learn more about building bridges foundation, visit www.building-b-foundationsproject.org. Marsha's enthusiasm about the power of God supersedes all of her shortcomings and her problems; because she knows that Jesus will fix it, after a while.